BRUNCH
IS
HELL

BRUNCH

IS

HELL

HOW TO SAVE THE WORLD
BY THROWING A DINNER PARTY

BRENDAN FRANCIS NEWNAM
AND RICO GAGLIANO

Illustrations by Fanny Blanc

Little, Brown and Company

NEW YORK BOSTON LONDON

Little, Brown and Company
Hachette Book Group
1290 Avenue of the Americas, New York, NY 10104
littlebrown.com

First Edition: December 2017

Little, Brown and Company is a division of Hachette Book Group, Inc.
The Little, Brown name and logo are trademarks of Hachette Book Group, Inc.

The publisher is not responsible for websites (or their content)
that are not owned by the publisher.

The Hachette Speakers Bureau provides a wide range of authors for speaking events.
To find out more, go to hachettespeakersbureau.com or call (866) 376-6591.

The Dinner Party Download® is an American Public Media production. All rights reserved.

Illustrations by Fanny Blanc

ISBN 978-0-316-33895-0
LCCN 2017951361

10 9 8 7 6 5 4 3 2

LSC-C

Printed in the United States of America

For Frank and Sandra Gagliano,

who taught me the beauty of music and laughter,

preferably enjoyed together

For Francis and Neda Newnam,

who taught me there is always room

for one more at the table

Table of Contents

BRUNCH
IS
HELL

BRUNCH IS HELL

A DINNER PARTY MANIFESTO

A specter is haunting America: the specter of brunch.

Brunch, the dissolute Minotaur: half breakfast, half lunch.

Brunch, singing siren songs of bacon, alcohol, and attractive-yet-aloof waitstaff.

"BRUNCH!!!" scream chalkboards propped up outside every restaurant and café, in every city in the Western world, every weekend morning.

What? You *don't* plan to brunch this Sunday morn-fternoon? Not to worry: your social media feeds will be rich with evidence of the rest of the world brunch-brunch-brunching away in your absence.

Behold! Photo after photo on social media of your smiling friends, lounging on sun-dappled restaurant patios, holding aloft plates heaped with smoked salmon tartines, savory waffles, and scrambles — always the scrambles.

How charming brunch seems!

What hell it actually is!

But you already know that. You are at this very moment holding a book called *Brunch Is Hell*. You've spent a full minute of your all-too-brief life reading these words. On some deep, instinctive level, you sense the malignancy of brunch. Perhaps you just *came* from brunch. Or perhaps you're in a bookstore, scanning these words through a post-brunch mimosa fog, your wallet lightened by eighteen bucks wasted on two eggs and a piece of toast. Your belly is full, yet you feel empty. *Spiritually* empty. Like, Dad's-promise-to-play-catch-with-you empty.

You know something is deeply wrong with brunch. Something you can't quite put your syrup-encrusted finger on.

Take heart. You're not crazy. We're about to explain the sick truth at the heart of this hybrid-meal menace. And we're going to prescribe the perfect antidote. It's called a dinner party.

★　★　★

TEN YEARS AGO, we launched a podcast called *The Dinner Party Download*, which only tangentially had anything to do with dinner parties. At first, all we wanted to create was an excuse to talk to the coolest artists in the world about anything we wanted, and to get booze and food for free. *The Brendan and Rico Talk to Awesome People and Drink and Eat for Free Show* seemed like a cumbersome title, though.

Then we realized that everything we wanted to cover in our little arts-and-leisure podcast was the sort of thing one might discuss at a dinner party: the latest and most interesting movies, TV, books, comedy, news, cocktails, and food. Plus, the concept of a dinner party provided us with a handy structure: each segment in the show would correspond to a phase of a dinner party! Great idea! *The Dinner Party Download* was born.

We didn't expect this organizing concept to define our careers. But over time, listeners (and publications from the *Wall Street Journal* and the *Chicago Tribune* to *Marie Claire*) came to us for the secrets to throwing great dinner parties. How to coax, from their own guests, the kind of thoughtful and/or witty conversations they heard on the show. What food to serve. How to mix drinks. How to tell a lame joke and not have people punch you in the mouth.

We started taking notes at parties: what made them interesting, or fun,

4

RICO GAGLIANO

or, at times, unmitigated dumpster fires. We developed strong opinions about dinner parties. Very strong opinions. *Very very* strong opinions. And we began to respect dinner parties. Far from their frivolous reputation, we realized, dinner parties, properly thrown, can serve as the very CORNERSTONE OF A HEALTHY MODERN SOCIETY, because they create happy and empathetic humans. And leftovers. Which, yum.

Alas, there's something rotten in the state of dinner parties. And it's not lutefisk.

It's that people aren't having enough of them anymore.

We hear this all the time from older listeners who say they're too busy or tired to throw dinner parties. Or from millennial listeners who confess that the closest they've *ever* come to throwing a dinner party is sharing Altoids with their roommates whilst making student loan payments over pirated Wi-Fi. A few years back, no less a journal than the *New York Times* documented the death of the dinner party, noting, "Informal gatherings occurring outside the home have largely replaced the dinner parties popular not long ago."

You know what "informal gatherings occurring outside the home" is a euphemism for, don't you? Fucking brunch, that's what.

*   ↑   ↓

"OKAY," you are wondering impatiently, having now spent *five* minutes of your day on this weird book, "so what exactly makes brunch anathema to a happy life and society? And why specifically should I care that it has displaced the dinner party from its once-exalted spot at the center of our civilization?"

You wonder this because you have not yet meditated upon our DINNER PARTY MANIFESTO. In it, we lay out the foundational principles that, when recognized and acted upon by all humankind, will create a joyful social existence, a fully functioning society...and just, like, nicer times, man.

A perfect dinner party is the purest expression and embodiment of these principles. Brunch is their fiendishly sinister antithesis, plus a small cup of fruit salad.[1]

Know these principles. Internalize them. Then we'll show you how to build upon them and take action, by planning your own dinner party. What's that you say? You feel weightless? That's because you just launched yourself over the barricades...into a revolution.

---

1   With, maybe, one raspberry in it.

THE DINNER PARTY MANIFESTO
EIGHT PRINCIPLES TO LIVE BY

#1

DON'T WASTE THE TIME YOU HAVE TO WASTE!

Leisure time must not be squandered.

All week, we toil at work, or network frantically in order to *find* some work. Finally comes some time off: At last, a little space for dreams to be realized! A few precious hours to explore the world, or each other, or the wonders inside our own minds! And what do we blow a big chunk of it on?

Brunch. Adulthood's booby prize. After brunch, any chance to use the day fruitfully has been drowned in hollandaise. Slouching out of the bacon hall long after noon, we are tired, heavy, and limp, like an overdressed side salad. That screenplay you were thinking of penning? It has been preempted by a Bloody Mary–fueled food coma. That hike with the kids you thought you were gonna take?[1] Yawn — you'll do it next weekend. (That is, if you're not seduced by *another freaking brunch*.)

Understand that we are not saying free time must be productive. Merely

---

1   Note to people with little kids or babies: You are forgiven the occasional restaurant brunch, as your evenings are typically consumed with feeding and bedtime drama, leaving brunch as the ideal (and perhaps only) time to drink and commiserate with fellow parents about little Rafael's penchant for peeing on iPads and/or daughter Zoe's Fig Newman–induced rages.

useful. Pointless silliness, for instance, is useful—indeed, it's essential for mental health (see principle three, below). But we *are* saying that after brunch, you won't be acting silly or doing much of anything else. Because at that point, your options will consist of a) lapsing into a drool-sleep or b) blearily watching TV whilst lightly moaning.

Luckily, there's an alternative, sitting on the opposite end of your day off. It comes *after* getting in the hike, painting your masterpiece, or having a giggly thumb war with your significant other. Unlike brunch, it can even come at the end of an office workday:

THE DINNER PARTY.

And when you're done throwing it, it's nighttime. The time you're *supposed* to be tired and maybe a little drunk. The time you're *supposed* to fall asleep.

#2
GIVE AND LET GIVE!

Humans must give and receive stuff for no reason at all.

The two greatest powers known to man are the power of *pure generosity*... and the power of *gratitude*.[2]

Your body *likes* it when you're generous. In fact, when you give, your brain floods your system with the same endorphins that provide runners with their notorious "high." Are you processing this? *The same high* as runners, without shredding your knees, or wearing those little shorts with the bathing suit lining!

Your body also likes to experience gratitude. Scientist Robert A.

---

2 There is also the power of napping, but we'll cover that in our forthcoming audiobook/sleep aid entitled *Boyfriends Talking About Their Favorite Records*.

Emmons studied a hundred thousand volunteers and learned that people who are truly grateful for what they receive enjoy: stronger immune systems, lower blood pressure, better sleep, more joy and pleasure, and more optimism and happiness. They also have a tendency to be more helpful, generous, compassionate, forgiving, and outgoing.

You will gain none of these superpowers from brunch.

Brunch involves ZERO giving or thankfulness. Brunch is an endless cycle of sadomasochism, sans sexy boots and knot-tying skills.

The brunchgoer plays the role of Master:

"Bring me water! And I'll take the fennel soufflé. But instead of fennel, make it with okra. And coat the ricotta zucchini blossoms with rice flour instead of *flour* flour. Fry it extra crispy. Serve all that before the French toast cheesesteak. Also: coffee, with almond milk, and if not almond milk, soy milk, and if not soy milk, black, like the leather fetish mask which I am currently imagining you wearing."

Meanwhile, the laborer plays Servant, paid subminimum wage to fulfill the whims of the Master. And they don't even get a safe word.

Of course, as in any such relationship, beneath the surface the *reverse* is also true. The order placed, the once-Dominant customer now becomes Submissive — immobilized at the table, helpless to enter the kitchen to oversee preparation of the meal, beholden to the Waiter/Master, without whose aid and attention the banana pancakes might not be served with warmed maple syrup . . . or indeed, served at all.

Do you sense Giving or Gratitude anywhere in that equation?

"But what of grat*uity?*" the brunch fan might remark. "Surely tipping is a generous act!" Really, now? The obligatory 20 percent? That's not a tip — it's mandatory payment for services rendered. If you fail to pay, good luck leaving brunchville without a server shivving you in the chest with a broken ketchup bottle.

"But what if my friend picks up my half of the check?" you might ask.

1s like a generous act of giving!" Ah, but is it? Tossing a credit
tray? This is the equivalent of breaking up with someone via text:
~~~~ ~~ ~~t of convenience than an act of virtue, a means of avoiding the
awkward math of check division. Besides, you know that buying brunch is
a ploy, right? Later, your "friend" will just expect you to pick up the dinner
check. Which is going to cost twice as much.

To recap: You are not grateful. And they are not giving, so much as
sowing the seeds for *taking*.

But lo — *witness the dinner party!* A truer embodiment of Give and Let
Give does not exist-eth!

The host — in an act of generosity second only to letting a stranger on
the highway merge without signaling — welcomes guests into his or her
most private space. Feeds them delicacies. Fills their glasses with euphoria-
inducing fermented grape juice. And then listens patiently when they complain about how Best Buy refused to allow them to combine a 20 percent off
coupon with the one-day-only sale price on that humidifier.

And in return for all this giving, the host receives something in return.
Because it turns out that when you give, your body produces not just the
aforementioned endorphins, but also the "love hormone," oxytocin. Which
by the way is the same biological process that occurs during sex. So a dinner
party is basically an orgy, without having to see your friend Brian's hairy
back.

What's more, this endor-xycontin cocktail — with, don't forget, some
wine dumped in there, too — renders you more empathetic and more con-
nected to others, and generally makes you a way better person than the
fatigued, stiff-necked, late-capitalism-blues-addled human you were when
the evening began.

And those are just the benefits to the *host!* That's the person who dislo-
cated his spine lugging home a leg of lamb in a tote bag, and who has to do
the dishes later! Think of the benefits to the grateful *guest*, who gets to eat

said lamb, and drink the wine, and experience all the ecstatic health benefits that come with feeling gratitude!

But if that sounds terrible to you for some reason, fine: give us your cell phone number and we'll call you when a table is ready. The approximate wait time is forever.

#3

STOP MAKING SENSE!

Humanity needs unstructured time to do ridiculous things.

This may seem counterintuitive. Surely mankind is at its best when logic, discipline, and rationality rule the day, right?

Yet in the most awesome eras of human civilization, extreme rationality coincided with extreme wackiness. Witness 1969, the year Americans put a man on the Moon...and then, a month later at Woodstock, dropped acid and humped in the mud until Jefferson Airplane's set actually sounded good.

It's not surprising that we're at our best when we mix the sane with the wild. Just as kids need unstructured playtime to thrive, adults need recess, too—like, literally *need* it. According to health-care providers, grown-ups can look forward to delightful stuff like stress headaches and high blood pressure if they don't do something unstructured every day.

Well, dinner parties are recess for adults.

Not a place absent of any rules at all—a civil place—but one where wildness can safely blossom. Where it's okay to have an extra drink. Flirt with someone you shouldn't. Talk loudly. Dance badly. Confess an ill-informed, mildly offensive thought. Ignore your diet. Smoke a joint if that's your poison, or do enough cocaine to remember why it's a bad idea to do cocaine. Brainstorm an opera. Or a manifesto about dinner parties. Or simply *be* in a space where you're not exactly sure what someone will do or say next.

Does any of this sound like what goes down at your local brunch spot? Other than the "Ignore your diet" part? Yes, you might drink, but at such an early hour that it's not lowering your *inhibitions* so much as your *eyelids*. Wanna whip out your guitar and improvise a ballad about filibusters or something? They'll kick you out and use the guitar as fuel for the wood-fired grill. And yeah, go ahead and spark a joint at the brunch table. You will then be arrested.[3]

There is no room, at brunch, for the freewheeling and the unstructured. It's a pile of spontaneity-killing restrictions and rules, with patio seating and eggs. It's a series of hoops through which society wants you, a trained monkey wearing a demeaning Shriner hat, to jump. Whereas a dinner party is where we get to SWAT THE HOOPS ASIDE and SWING FREELY FROM THE GOD-GIVEN TREES.

#4

PERFECT IMPERFECTION!

Humans must embrace what flawed, weird screwups we are.

Acting like we are perfect is, at worst, a fast track to disenchantment and disillusionment . . . and at best makes us feel *super stressed-out and uncomfortable.*

You are perhaps familiar with the term "the uncanny valley"; it's the revulsion we experience when confronted by something that looks very much human . . . but not *quite*. Example: Nadine — the "lifelike" android that engineers in Singapore hope will one day provide companionship to lonely elderly people. Riiight. Nadine resembles a person, but her movements are too precise, her smile too perfect, to actually be human. She lacks

---

3   Except in states with lax marijuana laws, where we admit that brunch is therefore way more fun.

unpredictable emotion. She lacks *im*perfection. We gaze uneasily upon her, knowing we'd never leave her alone with Grandpa, for fear she would dispassionately murder him.

WELL, BRUNCH IS THE "NADINE" OF HUMAN INTERACTIONS.

Witness: A scene at a typical fancy brunch spot. Isn't it *darling?* It is awash in flowers, each in perfect bloom, the ideal complement to the starched gingham tablecloths, on which sit matching gleaming place settings! The beautiful waitstaff serves you with quiet efficiency, urging you in hushed yet adorably conspiratorial tones to go ahead and have another Bloody Mary! "It's got a *wicked* kick, no?" beams your server, teeth sparkling in the warm patio light.

Yet all the while, there is that uncomfortable feeling. The sense that you have seen something like this scene before. In *THE STEPFORD WIVES*.

Or perhaps you're in a place like Brooklyn and the brunch spot is more ramshackle…but *expertly* ramshackle. The cocktails arrive in—oh, how *cute*—mismatched drinking vessels: a mason jar for you, a chipped teacup for your companion! The pulled pork hash is delivered in a blue plastic cereal bowl! And wait: what's that music on the sound system? "It's the first Ramones album," says your server through his lush beard, the tattoo on his neck pulsing as he pours you a seven-dollar Arnold Palmer.

Wow—Ramones, during *brunch?!* How *punk!*

Except it is *not* punk. It is the very definition of *POSEUR*. This brunch spot is a business machine, *mimicking* "ramshackle," doing its best to hide the gears of the profit-motivated robot grinding beneath that veneer of homespun humanity.

Don't get us wrong: It can be an entertaining experience to watch a machine attempt to appear human. But to regularly take part in the charade? To try and appear as though you, too, are a cog that belongs in this mechanism? That's going to sprain your fake-smile muscles, and kill your soul.

Ah, but at a dinner party like the ones we champion herein, the imperfect, the unpredictable, the flawed, and the wrong are *celebrated!*

Dinner parties are arranged and hosted by individual humans, who are not expected to be smiley and peppy no matter what happens. They might cuss and express an outrageous opinion, even.

They host the party in their real home. Which may not be spotlessly clean. Where, on your way to the bathroom, you might get a glimpse into their bedroom, strewn with undergarments and Chipwich wrappers. A real home, where the decor and the menu and the music are authentic reflections of the host's actual personality—not the end result of a data-crunched business plan.

At brunch, if the food arrives burned or bland, you complain and threaten to never return unless you're given a better quiche, or a refund. At a dinner party, if the food arrives burned or bland, you express sympathy and share a good laugh. Because, hey, we've all been there, and *nobody's perfect*.

Filmmaker Guillermo del Toro put it best on our show when he said,

> I am a lover of imperfection…only because it's a standard
> we can all live by, you know? I think imperfection is a
> highly attainable goal. Whereas perfection isn't. It isn't!…
> And I think when we allow ourselves to be imperfect,
> fallible, *grotesque*,[4] even, we deal with it.

---

4   He means "grotesque" metaphorically. You still have to clean your toilet before a dinner party (see chapter three).

TEND TO FRIENDS!

Humans must hang with groups of other humans with whom they neither work nor share genes.

That poster in your guidance counselor's office was right.

Not the one with the cat that says "Hang in there!" That poster is, in fact, wrong: the cat should stop torturing itself and let go. It's a cat, for God's sake. It'll totally land on its feet.

No, we're talking about that poster that touted the importance of friendship. Yes, wise poster: Friendship *Is* the Surest Way to Lasting Happiness.

But what makes friendship special is also what makes it, too often, a social afterthought: it's based on choice. Unlike work and family relationships, there are no immediate consequences for neglecting friendships.[5]

And it's not hard to fathom why friendships become so hard for the average grown-up to maintain. Peek at the typical person's to-do list:

<u>TO DO</u>
Thing for work
Thing for work
Family obligation
Thing for work
Cry
Work obligation
Thing for family
Family thing
(Repeat till dead)

---

5   Yes, an arid heart and a crushing sense of emptiness are consequences, but of a very different sort than, say, having no income or watching your daughter mistake a stranger for her father.

And maybe, at the end of a day, when the house is finally quiet, you log in to Facebook and scroll through pictures of people on vacation or losing hair or holding babies. Some of those people used to be your friends. Remember friends?

Work is important. Family is important. But your Life-Stool™ needs a third leg. That third leg is friendship. Your people. Your tribe. Without them, your life topples over.

We mean that almost literally: according to an exhaustive study conducted by the Gallup organization's Tom Rath, friendships improve health, save marriages, and help prevent you from becoming homeless.[6] Another study found that folks with a large network of friends lived longer than people with fewer friends. Like, *20 percent* longer.

And by the way, close relationships with children and relatives...had almost *no effect* on longevity.

Got that? Friends keep you alive. Whereas family members unilaterally remove your foreskin and hang that bucktoothed photo of you from third grade in the center of your living room.

So, friendship is necessary. But where in the twenty-four-hour call center of modern life do we cultivate new friendships and nurture old ones? The brunch spot? Where if you linger for more than an hour with your pals you're made painfully aware that you're costing the servers valuable tip money?

No. Brunch is for an obligatory meetup with cousins visiting from out of town, and your Mom says you *have* to go because she didn't raise a monster. As for making *new* friends, is the best time to do that with your face zigzagged with fresh pillow creases, and your breath redolent with the ripe scent of coffee and egg? That was a yes/no question, and the correct answer has two letters.

6   In fact, friends'll help you move *into* a home, if you buy them a six-pack.

People! The *dinner party* is the sanctuary of friendship. It is your secular church. Your secret meeting in the woods where everyone gets naked, sacrifices a bear, and then gets sexy time with each other in the bear's guts.[7] By the way, according to Brigham Young psych professor Julianne Holt-Lunstad, "Not having a social support network can be a higher death risk than obesity or leading a sedentary life without exercise." So we can say without equivocation that not having dinner parties will kill you.

#6
WELCOME STRANGERS!

We must spend time around people who are not exactly like us and who may even piss us off.

At your local brunch joint, do you encounter a broad cross section of society, representing a variety of social backgrounds and points of view? Or does the clientele consist of a whole bunch of YOUs, differentiated from one another only by the amount of sea salt they prefer on their avocado toast? We bet it's the latter.

And why wouldn't it be? As we've noted, the brunch joint is the result of a business plan designed to appeal to a demographic. If *you* like the place, the others in there likely share your taste in food, your interior design aesthetic, your coffee order, your newspaper of choice, your political biases, and perhaps in some cases your boyfriend.

Hell, even if your brunch spot *was* a social melting pot—perhaps *called* the Melting Pot—would you get up from your table to introduce yourself to the guy at the espresso counter wearing a Trump hat (or—for you

---

7   You guys do this too, right? Right?

Trump supporters — the coffee klatch of transgender fashion designers at the corner table)?

In a country becoming *physically* more polarized with each passing year, we doubt it. Liberals concentrate themselves in major cities and on the coasts; conservatives keep their distance in suburbs and the heartland. Between them yawns a vast chasm of desert, highway, and fashion sense that neither feels inclined to cross.

And even within these communities we *still* fear each other, probably thanks to nightly news reports showing us every violent crime in a twenty-mile radius. Studies say people who watch this stuff frequently are more likely to feel that their neighborhood is unsafe and that they'll be victimized at any moment. Now, admittedly, living in constant fear of The Other may spare you from, say, being shot by the trigger-happy vigilante next door who mistakes your evening walk for an assault on his creepy woodshed.[8] But fearing everyone *is how that guy got that way in the first place.* Think about it.

Furthermore, huddling for safety with people of your own kind actually prevents you from being as smart and creative as you could be. For real: "Decades of research by organizational scientists, psychologists, sociologists, economists, and demographers show that socially diverse groups...are more innovative than homogeneous groups."[9] That's straight from the pages of *Scientific American.* A magazine we trust, because the title consists of two words we fervently believe in.

So here's what you're gonna do. You're gonna roast up a chicken, buy some cheap wine...and then take any opportunity to make your guest list a veritable *rainbow of humanity.* The tribe we told you earlier to create? Strive to expand it with new members from *other* tribes.

8   Full of heavily annotated "evidence" that CNN is spying on him with robot fruit bats.
9   Katherine W. Phillips, "How Diversity Makes Us Smarter," *Scientific American,* Oct. 1, 2014.

When your pal tells you she'll come over just as soon as she ditches her Tea Party uncle... tell her to *bring him along*.

Your immigrant cabbie made you laugh? Put him on the guest list, too — and not just because you have a feeling he'll drive home your one pal who never can hold his liquor.

This is our idea of a dinner party: the metaphorical equivalent of pushing your table up against a stranger's at the brunch joint. Except without the stranger worrying you're on PCP. Or a server complaining that you're blocking the aisle.

#7

GET OFF-BRAND!

Humans need a safe space away from advertising's 24-7 soul assault.

Depending on which marketing researcher you ask, folks in the Western world get bombarded with an estimated 3,500 to 10,000 brand images a day. And not just on TV, where, for instance, Super Bowl ads are admittedly more entertaining than the game. Or in magazines, where you *expect* to thumb through fifty fragrant pages of Chanel ads before you get to that article about Prince William's parenting style. No, you're bombarded with ads pretty much all the time, *no matter what you do*.

The front window of your local watering hole is festooned with neon booze signs. The roadside on your drive to work is lined with billboards advertising new cars *and* personal injury lawyers to represent you when one of those cars crashes into you. Wanna show your pal a sweet ten-second YouTube video of a parrot massaging a cat? First you'll have to sit through a nerve-splintering *thirty*-second ad for a new horror film that's full of shrieking people with blood on their faces.

Hell, we know a guy with an image of Cap'n Crunch tattooed on his shoulder. Hook up with him and you'll experience a cereal ad *while having intercourse.*

According to a UK think tank called Compass, the effects of all this advertising range from turning kids into whiny little greed machines to making it increasingly difficult for adults to imagine a world "where time and relationships matter more than what we buy."

To remedy the situation, critics call for (among other things) a ban on advertising in all public spaces and levying a tax on all advertisers. Sounds great! As does a world in which unicorns pee IPA and smoking improves respiratory health. But until these impossible things happen, how do we take shelter from the consum-nami?

Probably not by driving down the billboard-packed street to a brunch spot, to sit at a sidewalk table beneath more billboards and order from a menu which boasts Blue Bottle Coffee™, Niman Ranch™ bacon, and Horizon™ organic milk. While the entire waitstaff is financially motivated to upsell you a bunch of stuff you can't afford and aren't really even hungry for, in a manner not unlike, oh... *advertising.*

No. The best we can do is create for ourselves, *and for each other,* a respite from the consumer blitz... in the form of, yes, dinner parties. We can welcome friends and neighbors into our homes and draw a blessed curtain between them and the billboards. We can serve them foods denuded of packaging, in an environment free of brands. We can short-circuit the ad machine by creating a space where the TV is off, and the only deceptive sales pitch is "C'mon, two more slices of caramel cheesecake won't kill you."[10]

---

10   RIP Uncle Jeffrey "Diabetes Fats" Newnam (1939–1995).

#8

LOVE!

Humans must avoid hate and experience love – duh.

Try this experiment: At around midnight, strip to your underwear, lie down in bed, close your eyes, and don't eat for eight hours. Wake up, get dressed, walk a mile to your local brunch spot, and stand in withering hot morning sun for an hour waiting to be seated. Enter a packed room where everyone's banging glasses and plates while shouting, as loud tinny music blares. Sit on a wooden chair. Stay there for ninety minutes. Leave all the cash you have on a tray. Walk home.

Now answer these questions.

If a jolly busker started performing in front of you, would you:

a) Toss him a coin? Or:
b) Sweep his legs and hog-tie him with his guitar strings?

If someone inadvertently cut you off in traffic, would you:

a) Take a deep breath and thank goodness you were safe? Or:
b) Pin the horn with your elbow while feeling under your seat for a bottle, rock, or loose D battery with which to penetrate the offending driver's rear window?

If you got a phone call from your mother, would you:

a) Answer and ask how her weekend's going? Or:
b) Immediately demand to know why she insists on ruining your life and relitigating every mistake you've made since fucking kindergarten?

Thought so. The truth is simple: Brunch breeds hate. True fact which is true:[11] Drafters of the Geneva convention designated "brunch" as a rare *non-war-crime* war crime. Only after ferocious lobbying by the World Mimosa Council and the International Federation of Hash Browns was the provision dropped.

Brunch breeds hate because brunch, by its nature, *is the absence of* love. True![12] This horrible day-destroying meal was only invented in the first place so restaurateurs could sell leftovers from the previous night's dinner service before it rotted. So brunch is *literally made of unloved things.* Sometimes even served *while* My Bloody Valentine's album *Loveless* is playing.

As Dostoyevsky wrote, "What is hell? I maintain that it is the suffering of being unable to love."[13]

By which he meant: *Brunch* is hell.

Guess where heaven, and love, reside? Hint: It rhymes with "Krinner Krarty."

*   *   *

"YOU'RE RIGHT!" you're thinking. "Now I understand that this burning angst in my chest isn't the jalapeño waffles I just consumed at brunch; *it's the concept of brunch itself!*" Your newly opened, non-daydrunk eyes blink in the hot white glare of Truth.

"And wait," you might now also rightly ask, "*why* isn't everyone throwing obviously glorious dinner parties?"

The short answer: Fear. A misguided dread of the perceived time-swallowing difficulty of throwing a party. Or an ill-informed fear that throwing a party requires some sort of training, or innate hosting "gift." Or just plain social anxiety, which keeps perfectly awesome people from host-

---

11   Not true.

12   *Actually* true.

13   *The Brothers Karamazov,* chapter forty-one.

ing the dinner parties they were born to host, and which humankind desperately needs.

Hence the remainder of this book: a detailed guide to hosting a dinner party, from guest list to subpoena. Keep reading, and you'll see there's no need to fear the dinner party. We're anti perfectly executed meals, anti planning, anti project management, and anti spending tons of money. This is not rocket science for millionaires. It is, in fact, *fun*.

Mainly we aim to let you know what to expect as your party hums along, to provide you with some helpful tips and some tales to tell…and most of all to set minimum standards of behavior to which hosts and guests can aspire. Partly because we're sick of some of the nonsense that people, *including ourselves,* pull at dinner parties. But mainly because if we all adhered to some standards, everyone would enjoy dinner parties more and throw a ton more of them.

And when you all do, we hope you'll then invite us over. Because honestly, now that we're finished writing this book, our lives feel empty.

Read on, and change the world forever.

 DINNER PARTIES THAT ACTUALLY DID CHANGE THE WORLD

30ISH A.D.: THE LAST SUPPER

Naturally, someone as cool as Jesus would, in pretty much his last act as a free man, have some pals over for dinner. It wasn't exactly a playful gathering, of course: Jesus used it as an opportunity to prophesize his own betrayal and prepare the apostles for his death. He could get away with that kind of a downer moment at a shindig, though; we recommend that *you* keep the mood a tad lighter.

1790: DC FOUNDED OVER DINNER

So Thomas Jefferson bumps into Alexander Hamilton outside George Washington's pad. No, that's not the setup of a joke — but it *was* an important moment in dinner party (and American) history. Apparently, T. J. invited Hamilton over for dinner that night…and *also* put Hamilton's archnemesis, James Madison, on the guest list. During the course of the meal, the two politicians put aside their differences and struck a deal to, among other things, make Washington, DC, our nation's capital. See what happens when you bring opposing tribes together over some nice ratatouille?[14]

1816: A DINNER PARTY SPAWNS A MONSTER

Teenage author Mary Shelley and her main squeeze, Percy Bysshe, spent the summer of '16 at poet Lord Byron's pad in Switzerland. One night, drinking and dining around a crackling fire, they started

---

14   Jefferson — a notorious Francophile — very likely served his guests French cuisine. Ironic, considering the "Freedom fries" thing that swept DC in the aughties.

reading to one another from a book of German ghost stories. This gave Mary nightmares...one of which she then turned into a little novel called *Frankenstein,* basically inventing a whole new horror genre in the process. Moral of the story: Always have a book of German ghost stories near the dinner table.[15]

1966: CHILDREN'S MINDS ENRICHED, WITH HELP FROM MARTINIS

According to TV producer Joan Ganz Cooney, *Sesame Street* was created over the course of a midcentury dinner party at her New York apartment. One of the attendees, a big shot at the Carnegie Foundation, kept complaining about his three-year-old kid's utter addiction to TV. The folks at the party talked it over and realized, hey: if the kids'll watch *anything* on the tube, why not put a show on there that would actually *educate* them in the process? Yes, fast-food entrepreneurs: if it wasn't for that party, Big Bird might still be available as a name for your fried chicken chains.

---

15   Crackling fire optional. Also, make sure you invite someone who can translate German.

CHAPTER ONE

WHAT IS A DINNER PARTY?

Before committing yourself to our dinner party blueprint, you should first figure out if the gathering you plan to host *is*, in fact, a dinner party. Because while the definition of a dinner party may self-evidently seem to be "a party which occurs over dinner," the truth, as with most things of world-shaking importance, is a little more complex. For example:

- Is it a dinner party if you're eating at 4 p.m.?
- Is Passover seder a dinner party?
- What if the food is takeout pizza and the booze comes in shiny twelve-ounce pull-tab cans with a contest advertised on the back?

These are all potentially swell gatherings. But none of them are dinner parties, and in this chapter, we're going to tell you why.

PART 1: MINIMUM STANDARDS

Below are the internationally recognized standards which define the modern dinner party, as put forth by the UN Nutrition and Reverie Commission's Subcommittee on Common Sense. A.k.a. us. In ensuing chapters, you'll see, we advocate a casual disregard for many rules. But a true dinner party must at least adhere to these basic standards for it to qualify for the revolution.

1. The purpose of throwing a dinner party is to have dinner and to party.

A dinner party must have *no agenda* other than this. As explained in the MANIFESTO, our lives are already planned enough; the dinner party is a space for spontaneity. It is, as we will remind you several more times throughout the course of this tome, *recess for adults*. When you were a kid, did you actually *plan* to get beaten up at recess? No! It just kind of happened. Dinner parties are like that, except instead of randomly getting beaten up, random fun occurs.

TIME

1. Weekday dinner parties must begin after 5 p.m.

A true dinner party begins after the typical workday has ended, i.e., *no earlier than* 5 p.m. This is so a maximum number of invitees can actually attend.

It's also because a dinner party should be a *celebration* of time away from work. Not a burden that forces guests to abandon work early, fight rush hour traffic, and then spend the whole party worrying about the work they didn't do.

In fact, rule of thumb: Begin the party a half hour *later* than your town's typical rush hour *ends*. So, for instance, in Los Angeles, that'd be about midnight.

2. Weekend dinner parties must **also** begin after 5 p.m.

This allows enough time for the following:

   a) For hosts to sleep late, and then clean the bathroom for the party.
   b) For guests to sleep late, do one chore, and then do something fun, productive, or otherwise excellent for themselves before the party (e.g., hiking, sex, sitting quietly and enjoying trees).

c) For guests to buy some booze to bring to the party.

Another reason dinner parties happen after 5 p.m. is because that's when *dinner* happens, guys.

3. There is no standard end time for a dinner party.

You're thinking of *children's* parties. Those have end times so parents know when to pick up their kids from your house, with a few hours to spare to get them ready for bed.

A grown-up may also have a bedtime, but the awesome part about being a grown-up is you're allowed to blow it off. A dinner party is only over when the last guest leaves/drunkenly stumbles into a cab.

> 3a. HOWEVER, if some or all of your dinner party guests end up sleeping over, then the party officially ends at dawn. In other words, *the ensuing gathering the next morning is no longer a dinner party.* It is breakfast. With a very real danger (due to the proximity of leftover food and booze) of brunch breaking out. Be on guard.

DAY OF THE WEEK

1. Dinner parties must NOT be held on Sundays, Mondays, or Tuesdays.

You and/or at least some of your guests have to work on Monday. Not even the most magical Sunday night party can make someone forget how much that sucks. Don't bother trying.[1]

As for Monday nights, they are for doing stuff you thought you'd do

---

1   Exception: If Monday is a day off due to a minor holiday (e.g., President's Day), Sunday can be treated as a "bonus Saturday" and therefore fair game for a dinner party.

over the weekend, but didn't, because it felt too much like work. Like paying bills, or writing a book about dinner parties.

Tuesday nights are just kind of dumb.

2. Fridays and Saturdays are the optimal nights for a dinner party.

Both Fridays and Saturdays are part of that brief weekend window during which you can trick yourself into thinking you've escaped the rat race. Each is also followed by a convenient twenty-four-to-forty-eight-hour hangover/humiliation recovery period.

Be aware, however, that for these very reasons, 50 to 100 percent of your friends will be throwing various types of parties on Friday or Saturday nights. Competition for guests will be fierce. Therefore:

3. Wednesday and Thursday night dinner parties are encouraged.

By Wednesday or Thursday night, it's been long enough since you've been at a party to feel like being at another one. And partying on a "school night" is a great way to celebrate the freedoms of adulthood.

What's more, a great Wednesday or Thursday night dinner party can effectively "front-load" your weekly allotment of social time. This leaves you Friday and Saturday night to read, relax, or fall down an Instagram hole while everyone else sits in traffic on their way to parties.

4. Holidays

Parties held during the week preceding a major national holiday are not dinner parties. They are *holiday* parties (see part two, subsection "Holiday Parties").

LOCATION

1. For the time being, a dinner party must happen on the planet Earth.

We cannot advocate the consumption of large quantities of wine in the zero gravity environment of the International Space Station.

2. A dinner party must be held at a private residence.

Or a public residence, if your home is the White House. 'Cause, hey, you spent a lot of money in order to live there.

Now then: why a private residence, as opposed to a public spot? Partly because the cops are a lot less likely to intervene if anyone gets loud or naked. But also because welcoming non-family-members into your home is the most civilized of all possible acts. When Thorag invited Grunt over for pterodactyl sous vide, trusting that Grunt would not club him in the face and then eat Thorag's wife, Lauren — well, that was a big step for mankind. As best-selling author and military documentarian Sebastian Junger once told us on our show,

> Humans are the only species in which a young male (or
> female, for that matter)...will sacrifice his own life
> defending a peer he is not related to.

Swap "sacrifice his own life defending" with "give his last piece of roast beef to," and you've got the idea. Being a host to your pals = humanity.

To summarize thus far: A dinner party is a gathering held on Earth, after 5 p.m., Wednesdays through Saturdays, in someone's home, at which pterodactyl is served. Speaking of which:

1. A proportion of the food at a dinner party must be homemade.

Not cooking for your own dinner party is like DJ-ing a dance party with the radio. As clearly stated in our MANIFESTO, the point of a dinner party is to revel in unique, gloriously imperfect humanity. *Your* humanity. Expressing *your* taste, *your* style, and *your* essence, with food you prepared with your own hands, is part of what makes this deal so important.

The preparation of food also serves as the narrative spine of your event: cooking, serving, and cleanup are the three acts of your gathering. Without them, a dinner party is a movie without a plot. That only works for Richard Linklater.

2. The 51 percent rule.

DON'T WORRY. We acknowledge the distractions and pressures of the modern world, where whole seasons of binge-worthy TV shows are released daily, and where your boss can text you work tasks even while you're in labor. You may not have a ton of extra time to cook a multicourse meal. Therefore, a gathering is a dinner party *as long as at least 51 percent of the dishes served are made at home.*

This means that yes, you can serve a bunch of killer tamales you ordered from that great Mexican place down the street. *But you must additionally prepare a salad and your mother's special* queso *recipe.* And bake cookies for dessert or something. Also:

3. Hide the packaging.

At a true dinner party, all non-homemade food is removed from its packaging. If you serve the tamales straight out of the giant foil pan in which they were delivered, for instance, that's not a dinner party, that's a feeding trough. Just put the tamales on some kind of serving dish, would you? Even piling them up on a dinner plate like a meat-and-masa ziggurat is acceptable.

This rule goes double for food packaging emblazoned with a corporate logo. Remember, *dinner parties are a respite from advertising.* Your dining room is not a billboard, and your gathering is not a Hollywood blockbuster—this is no time for product placement.

ENVIRONMENT

1. Mandatory table.

For a gathering to qualify as a dinner party, there must be a table present.

> 1a. The table's purpose is to force the entire group to converse together; therefore, attendees *must actually be seated around it while dining.*

2. A dinner party is an A/V-free zone.

All audiovisual electronic equipment within twenty-five yards of a dinner party must be switched off—except for the minimum amount necessary to play music. The goal is to keep visual distractions to a minimum so the focus is on the *humans sitting in front of you.*

Thus, your television is subject to the same rule that applies to you when visiting your attractive doctor: It should not be turned on. A Super Bowl viewing party is not a dinner party.

Cell phone usage should be tightly policed. A quick hourly check of mail/messages is cool, but guests attempting to launch YouTube (see box "A History of Threats: What the Dinner Party Has Survived") should be denied food/booze and mocked until they desist. Otherwise your dinner party will quickly become a YouTube party.

For the same reason, laptops are verboten unless they are your music source.

Also, disable all Roombas. They're cute—everyone will look at them.

3. A dinner party can be held outside.

Among the most iconic dinner parties ever is the alfresco gathering in Fellini's Italian cinema classic *8½*.[2] Indeed, between April and August in many European countries, dinner parties are held indoors only in the event of hail or war. So by all means, set up a table in the backyard! Just take care you're not accidentally throwing a barbecue, which is a totally different thing (see part two, subsection "Outdoor Barbecues").

ATTENDEES

1. The four-to-twelve rule.

To qualify as a dinner party, your guest list must include *at least* four people but *no more than* twelve. That's including you, the host.

Two people is just dinner: quiet and comfortable. It's a pair of friends sharing a meal. It's you and your spouse catching up after a long day. Add a third person, and there's a tendency for things to turn into something more like therapy than a party. It's a sympathetic couple keeping their sad single friend sane. Or three single friends venting about condescending couples.

Four people *can* comprise a dinner party, unless the attendees are two couples, in which case it's no longer a dinner party and becomes a double date (see part two, subsection "Double Dates").

As for a guest list of more than twelve people? You'll have a hard time fitting them all around one table. It'll get too loud for everyone to ever share

---

2   True, that party had, like, a thousand guests, in clear violation of the four-to-twelve rule (see part one, subsection "Attendees"). But when you're among the greatest filmmakers of all time, you can file for an exception.

one conversation. And making enough salad for that many guests is going to give your salad-tossing arm carpal tunnel. If your guest list exceeds twelve people, just put out cheese and crackers and call your gathering a plain old party, which is what it is.

2. Family members: The 25 percent rule.

As clearly stated in our MANIFESTO, dinner parties are an essential means of maintaining and cultivating friendships *outside* your family. Therefore, your gathering is not a dinner party *if more than 25 percent of the attendees are your relatives.* Family gatherings can be great, but at a dinner party the majority of guests should be there because they *choose* to be—not because they're obligated due to shared DNA.

Also, an overabundance of family members runs counter to the spirit of unencumbered, free-flowing conversation that is central to a dinner party. Which sibling did Mom love best? Why do you always get your way? Who punched the dachshund that one time? Such questions lurk beneath a family gathering like the NSA lurks beneath your web browser. Better to leave this Freudian morass for Thanksgiving.

PART 2:
WHAT IS NOT A DINNER PARTY

Now that we have laid out the above standards, which are absolutely immutable laws of the universe except when they're not (see part three, "Exceptions"), let's apply them to a series of other types of social gatherings, as a means to explain why they are *not* dinner parties.

DINING OUT WITH FRIENDS

Surely meeting a bunch of people at a restaurant qualifies as a dinner party, right? You've got tables, food, a dining area free of TV sets, and many restaurants don't even open until 5 or 6 p.m., in observation of the Time rule above.

But remember: zero percent of the food on a restaurant table was cooked at home, a violation of the Food rule (part one, subsection "Food").

And more importantly, dining at a restaurant is not an intimate demonstration of the human capacity for civility (as outlined in the Location rule [part one, subsection "Location"]). It is a public act in a place of business. Which is also anathema to the true, dinner party–style spontaneity we articulated in our MANIFESTO. Can you tell your server to crank up the music, dude, because this is your jam? Can you break out a Yahtzee board at the restaurant? Can you play a tepid round of strip poker, or even an ironic game of quarters?

If you're in a restaurant, and the answers to the above questions are all "Yes," you may be confusing the café attached to your youth hostel with a restaurant. Neither can house a dinner party.

POTLUCKS/BUFFETS

A potluck or buffet is *almost* a dinner party. But it is disqualified because the dining table is typically completely covered with platters of food. This forces guests to eat while standing, in violation of the Environment rule (part one, subsection "Environment").

A standing party discourages shared group conversation of more than a few people. It also makes eating a chore. In France (a founding member and cochair of the International Dinner Party Security Council), holding a plate of salmon and couscous for hours, unable to actually eat it because you're holding a drink in your *other* hand, is considered torture—a crime punishable by making you hold a plate of salmon and couscous for hours while holding a drink in your other hand.

Note, however, that if there are *two* tables present at the buffet—one upon which food is placed, and another around which guests sit and eat—

then this is not in fact a buffet. It's a dinner party with too much food for one table. Well done!

OUTDOOR BARBECUES

What's not to love about barbecues? Charred meat, swimming, day drinking, sunshine, day drinking, and day drinking. Unfortunately, the "sunshine" part means that a barbecue generally happens before 5 p.m., in clear violation of the Time rule (part one, subsection "Time"). And one doesn't tend to eat around a table at a barbecue, unless you consider the lip of a swimming pool a table.

As for day drinking, that sounds dangerously brunchy to us.

Furthermore, while dinner parties can be casual affairs, barbecues take it a step further: people wander randomly in and out of the house; squirt guns are tolerated at the table; it's totally acceptable to eat while wearing sunglasses. If dinner parties are concerts, a barbecue is more like a jam session. Of course, if you're into jam bands, you're now confused, because "jam" and "concert" mean exactly the same thing to you. But you likely also think peanut butter and honey sandwiches are a main course—so we're not sure dinner parties are your vibe anyway.

Tip: Barbecues can be fine places to *recover* from dinner parties.

PICNICS

Picnics tend to happen in public spaces, in violation of the Location rule (part one, subsection "Location").

Picnics also don't have tables. To which you might understandably exclaim, "Wait! Then what the hell do you call a PICNIC TABLE?" To which we reply: "Picnic table" is an oxymoron, along the lines of "vodka martini," "holy war," and "bad sex." A true picnic happens not around a table, but on the ground. On a blanket. With your friends. Whereas so-called picnic tables are what you carve your initials into while eating smashed, disturbingly warm ham sandwiches outside a public rest area in the midst of a road trip with your parents. Or the thing upon which you eat cold fried chicken while trying to avoid getting beaned with Frisbees at your nephew's birthday party in the park.

We can imagine a dinner party consisting of a gathering of friends in a *private* backyard, arranged around a picnic blanket which *symbolically* serves as a table. But for the most part, picnics aren't dinner parties; they are the little sister of barbecues.

P.S.: We have yet to see a portable wet bar that does the job.

PIZZA PARTIES

In Food, above, we allowed for the presence of some non-homemade, delivered food at a party. But delivered pizza seems, to us, a special case.

Maybe it's because, practically speaking, you pretty much *have* to serve pizza straight from the delivery box, in clear violation of the Food rule (part one, subsection "Food"), which requires you to remove premade food from its container. Of course, you might happen to have multiple extra-large pizza trays in your house from which to serve the pizza. But seriously, what kind of person has multiple extra-large pizza trays in the house, when you can just serve pizza straight from the delivery box?

Maybe it's because we can't help but associate pizza with our earliest, not entirely sophisticated stabs at party throwing: junior high sleepovers at which everyone gorged on Domino's, Jolt Cola, and Pringles till we threw up all over our *Cracked* magazines.

Whatever. Our position remains: A pizza party is not a dinner party. It's the backup plan if you burn the *homemade* pizza you were making for the dinner party.

CLUB MEETINGS

A club meeting can look a lot like a dinner party. Example: Your book club comes over to meet at your pad. Everyone sits around your dining room table and consumes a tasty homemade dinner you prepared. Meanwhile, you all talk about books—sometimes even *naughty* ones. Sounds like a dinner party to us!

Except for the unfortunate fact that your gathering has a prearranged agenda, thereby violating the Agenda rule, a.k.a. THE FIRST RULE OF A DINNER PARTY.

At a dinner party, you can talk about anything. Whereas if some folks at the book club meeting grow weary of talking about books? Tough: You're expected to talk about books anyway, *because it's a meeting of the book club.*

Of course, you could decide to abandon your club agenda. And in the above scenario, the moment you do, you'll be having a dinner party. At least until someone inevitably ruins everything by saying, "Wait a second: aren't we supposed to be talking about *The Goldfinch*?"

Tip: Club meetings can create great conversation fodder to deploy later in the week, when you're at an actual dinner party.

POKER NIGHTS

Though it takes place around a table at a buddy's pad, usually on a weekend, sometimes with homemade food on hand…there is, alas, an agenda on poker night: to take your friends' money while avoiding your family and masking your alcoholism as recreational drinking. Therefore, not a dinner party.

DOUBLE DATES

Again, even if your double date occurs in a private home over dinner, there is an agenda: to subtly flirt with your friend's date, thereby reminding your own date that you are funny and attractive. Not a dinner party.

OSCAR PARTIES

Involves watching TV on a Sunday night. Serve all the fancy food and booze you want: it's still not a dinner party.

A holiday party cannot be a dinner party, even if you manage to avoid the many pitfalls that would immediately disqualify it.

Like, let's assume yours is among the .0001 percent of holiday parties that is not a cheese-log-festooned buffet (see "Potlucks/Buffets," above). Let's also assume you've managed to throw this holiday party without inviting a large number of family members. And you've kept the guest list to a dozen or fewer people.

Firstly, dude, this is kind of a pathetic holiday party—where are all your friends and family, and where's the cheese log buffet? And second, it's still not a dinner party.

One of the main reasons to throw a dinner party is to make a typical week *a*typical. To add a night of bright spontaneity to the otherwise ho-hum workaday routine. Remember, as a kid, how excited you'd be for Halloween, Thanksgiving, or Christmas? Some time off from schoolwork, lots of food, a chance to relax? That's exactly how adults should feel before a dinner party.

But on *actual* Halloween, Thanksgiving, and Christmas, you don't need to create that feeling. *It's already there.* Parties, food, and relaxation are *assumed.* So to throw a dinner party during holiday season would be like taking your kids out for ice cream sundaes on Halloween. It'd be like having a birthday party on Christmas when you're not Jesus. It'd be like taking a nap while napping.

Actually, nap napping sounds kind of great. But the point is, the presence of a holiday nullifies the dinner party–ness of a dinner party, and renders it simply a party that is happening on a holiday.

PASSOVER SEDER

Despite being a wonderful ritual, and despite taking place around a table over dinner, Passover seders are not dinner parties. They are a hybridization of holiday party and book club meeting, at which the agenda is to read and discuss the Haggadah.

We also cannot sanction as a dinner party any gathering at which heavenly brisket is sitting in the oven, like, ten feet away, but you're not allowed to have any until you've sung one thousand verses of "Dayenu."

PART 3: EXCEPTIONS

This is a party guide, not Apple's Terms of Service. We are not unyielding corporate lawyers, although we do like their shoes. So let us ease your fears and acknowledge a few situations where the rules go out the window.

UNEMPLOYMENT/POVERTY

If you currently have little or no income, can barely afford food to cook, had to pawn your dinner table to make rent, and *still* want to have people over to eat a little something and converse? Then you are a hero trying to make the best of a dire situation, and you are free to do it any way you can manage.

Throw your dinner party anytime, on any day of the week you want. Sit on the floor dipping saltines into an open can of StarKist tuna, water down your last finger of Two-Buck Chuck so you have enough to pour each guest a juice glass full, and enjoy. Actually, write us, and we'll contribute a paper tablecloth you can put down to keep from staining the rug. Godspeed to you!

Note: The unemployment exemption does NOT apply if you're a member of the idle rich. Or if you're, like, on unpaid summer hiatus from your lucrative gig as the showrunner of a hit TV sitcom. Yes, you're not technically *earning* money, but you *have* it, cheater. Buy a freaking dinner table!

DORM ROOM/EFFICIENCY APARTMENT

If you reside in a space barely large enough to fit a bed, a microwave, a space heater, and a fire alarm, you are absolved from the need for a table. The point of the table is to get everyone huddled intimately together anyway, and you've accomplished this simply by squeezing them into your microscopic chicken pen of a home. This is also known as the I-Live-in-New-York-Paris-or-Amsterdam rule.

Since you have no kitchen, you are also absolved of having to serve homemade food, especially if you are a student dorm resident whose entire circle of friends *also* live in dorms, making it impossible to cook something in advance at one of their pads.

However, before serving, you must still remove food from its packaging. And your head and face from the hood of your sweatshirt.

FOREIGN COUNTRIES

The Time and Day rules can be flexible, depending on where you live.

Example 1: You live in Finland. It is late December and the sun doesn't rise for months on end. To maintain a faint glimmer of joy in your dark existence, you need as many dinner parties in your life as possible. Go ahead and throw one on a Monday or Tuesday night. Please—we beg of you.

Example 2: In Spain, the central meal of your day occurs at noon, and you get several hours off to enjoy it. Thus a dinner party can conceivably be held in the middle of the day, and also, we're jealous of you, and you're the home of Bea, an exchange student with whom Brendan attended high school and who broke his heart, and look, Bea, now Brendan's cowriting a book, so you and he should really catch up, and by the way he's not allergic to ketchup anymore.

A HISTORY OF THREATS:
WHAT THE DINNER PARTY HAS SURVIVED

Like the American buffalo and the Rolling Stones, the dinner party has proven itself to be remarkably resilient, even in what seemed like hostile historical environments. Here's an admittedly partial time-line of the challenges dinner parties have surmounted.

397,895 B.C.: FIRE INVENTED

"Wait," you say. "Didn't the invention of fire make dinner parties *possible?* People could actually hang out and enjoy themselves at night instead of cowering in the dark for fear of being torn apart by bear-size hyenas."

True. But the very gatherings made possible by fire wound up consisting of everybody just sitting around, staring dumbly at the pretty fire. It wasn't until someone got the idea to *obscure* the fire by cooking some hyena meat over it that rudimentary dinner parties were born.

FIRST CENTURY A.D.: THE FIRST TAKEOUT

In the ancient city of Pompeii, historians have found evidence of *thermopolia* — takeout stands where food was purchased to be eaten later at home. These were apparently so popular that eventually, even large Pompeiian homes rarely had kitchens or dining rooms,[3] making dinner parties impossible.

This, not surprisingly, drew the ire of the Roman gods,[4] who buried the city in volcanic ash. Upside: Italians got the message and are now the bestest home cooks ever.

---

3   True fact.
4   False fact.

LATE 1800S: TENEMENT LIVING

At the turn of the century, a great wave of European immigrants brought wonderful things to America: their cuisine, their strong work ethic, their rich cultural heritage. But with entire extended families forced to live almost literally on top of each other in crowded tenement apartment buildings, they also nearly brought about the end of the dinner party — as it became physically impossible to host a gathering with 25 percent or fewer relatives present.

JULY 12, 1908: THE BIRTH OF MILTON BERLE

An innocuous enough event at the time. But Berle would go on to host *Texaco Star Theater*, a television show so popular that a majority of Americans would stop everything to watch it. Since dinner parties cannot occur within twenty-five yards of an active TV, this reduced the number of potential dinner party nights per week from five to four — a whopping 20 percent decline! Thankfully, NBC canceled the show in 1956.

MAY 25, 1979: *ALIEN* RELEASED

In the sci-fi horror film's signature "chestburster" scene, a baby alien explodes out of John Hurt's chest in the middle of a friendly dinner gathering. This made people fear friendly dinner gatherings for much of the 1980s. Instead, they did something that makes you blissfully forget all about eating: cocaine.

1994: GEORGE FOREMAN GRILL INTRODUCED

With the advent of the boxing-champion-endorsed George Foreman Grill, macho cooking culture exploded. Men who had previously never even deigned to boil rice suddenly got way into the idea of cooking Baked Alaska–level dishes with specialized kitchen gear. Friendly dinner parties became tense (and costly) arms races, designed mainly to show off the host's impressive new piece of nuclear-powered food gadgetry.

It was not until men discovered that no machine exists to relieve the tedium involved with deveining shrimp or stirring risotto that they — and dinner parties — chilled the hell out.

FEBRUARY 14, 2005: YOUTUBE FOUNDED
JUNE 29, 2007: IPHONE RELEASED

The first put an endless universe of cat videos just a search term away. The second made it easy to stream them all at the table. Frankly, the dinner party has yet to fully recover.

CHAPTER TWO

INVITATIONS

M ost folks never quite get around to taking the first step toward throwing a dinner party: inviting people over.

The reason, as we've stated, is fear.

Fear of people, perhaps. Their opinions of you, your home, your food. Fear that you'll say or do something embarrassing. Or just generally the fear that OHMIGODEVERYTHINGWON'TBEPERFECT.

We understand. People can be weird. And there's an entire home entertaining *industry*, with a business model based on setting the bar for dinner party perfection impossibly high. Read an issue of *Martha Stewart Living* and you could be forgiven for thinking you're not allowed to throw a party unless you've woven each guest their own monogrammed quilt out of your own hair. Heck, we just laid a whole chapter of dinner party regulations on you! It's downright daunting.

Which we're sure is exactly how the brunch industrial complex likes it: a nation of cowering sheep too afraid to invite people over to *their own homes*. Better to let the brunch people help. Yes, much safer.

But here's the golden rule about dinner party rules: Ultimately, NOBODY CARES. You're inviting people over for free food and drinks. It's pretty much social bribery. Will they really get uptight about your paucity of salad forks? Or because you disobeyed us and ordered a pizza for your main course? They will not. *We'll* get uptight about the latter, but that's our *job*.

Furthermore, as we declared righteously in our MANIFESTO, one of the main reasons to throw a dinner party is to bust through the mistrust of others that's been bred into us by local TV news and AM radio. Being brave enough to invite people over, weird as they are, is an act of RIGHTEOUS DEFIANCE and SOCIAL GOOD.

Therefore, we say: Speak before you think. Make the leap and extend a party invitation as soon as it occurs to you. Like, right now. To both your best friends *and* to people you've barely met. Even if you don't have matching fabric napkins. Even if the recycling bin isn't emptied, or your laundry pile has grown to Blob-like proportions and taken your cat hostage. Your party will be taking place at night, so the light will be dim—no one will notice you haven't dusted. You can tell them the cat is on vacation in Maui.[1]

That being said, you might want to know how best to *extend* an invitation. You might want to be aware of the classic guest archetypes, and what mix thereof might result in maximum party excellence. This chapter contains all that essential information, plus jokes and stuff.

PART 1: HOW TO INVITE

Every single week someone asks us some version of the question "How do you get such great guests on your show?"

To which we *want* to answer, "That's surprising to you? Our show is fucking awesome—that's how." But then we remember that cussing out a public radio listener isn't the best way to get them to contribute during a pledge drive, and instead we tell them this story:

---

1   You can pronounce it "Meow-i," but be prepared for someone to strangle you with a lei.

Back in the late aughties, we were but midlevel reporters and producers on the public radio business show *Marketplace*. And each night, after listening intently for the telltale rustle of corduroy pants—a sure indication that our colleagues were leaving the office for the day—we'd sneak into the famed Frank Stanton Studios to construct what was then a tiny pet project: a podcast we were calling *The Dinner Party Download*.

The problem: How were we supposed to convince great musicians, authors, filmmakers, artists, and other cultural heavyweights to be guests on said podcast, which by the way no one had ever heard of?

Turns out: *by asking them.*

Yes, our first guest of honor was "nerdcore hip-hop" progenitor MC Frontalot, who happened to be Rico's pal and owed us a favor.[2] But we were soon extending invitations to people we really had no reason to believe would respond. Like *Trainspotting* author Irvine Welsh. Or handsome-devil (and Austin Powers nemesis) actor Robert Wagner.

Amazingly, they all came on the show. Despite the fact that we had an audience of approximately zero people. Despite the fact that, at the time, most people didn't know what a "podcast" even was. And despite the fact that the very *word* "podcast" is one of the lamest ever devised to describe a form of media. Seriously: it sounds like a farming technique.

They showed up because it sounded like fun, because they had the time, and because they liked talking to people and had stuff they wanted to say. The same goes for anyone who'd show up at your party.

So how do you invite people over? Step one: ASK THEM. You'll be surprised who says yes. Who knows? Maybe the Obamas were gonna spend the night chilling at home, but now that you mention it, hanging out with

---

2   Your secret[2a] is safe with us, Front.

2a (he killed a guy)

you over peel-'n'-eat shrimps and banana cream pie[3] sounds like just the thing.

Of course, in our complex modern world, the phrase "ask someone to come over" isn't as simple as it sounds. There are an ever-multiplying plethora of methods and mediums through which to extend an invitation to a dinner party and a few details that it's important to express on an invite. Allow us to simplify it all for you.

THE INVITE: A FEW DOS AND DON'TS

1. DO put the word "dinner" before "party."

You'd be surprised how many people send out invites to a party and forget to note that the central activity will be *dinner*. If your guests aren't given this essential piece of information, they may eat beforehand. Not good. Worse yet, if they think they're attending a regular old party, they might not bring wine (and all dinner party guests *must bring wine*—see chapter four).

2. DO request an RSVP.

You're cooking for people. You have the right to know how many you're cooking for, and how many chairs you'll need to squeeze around the dinner table. Yes, in the modern world, a surprising number of your guests will be jerkweeds who never RSVP (see box "A Note to Guests"). But asking for an RSVP regardless covers your ass, so if they show up anyway and have to eat the last remaining chicken wing while sitting on the floor, it's their own dumb fault.

---

3   Chef Bobby Flay once told us the ex-president "thinks of himself as a pretty good baker—he makes a good banana cream pie, apparently." So, should the Obamas accept your invite, make them bring a banana cream pie.

3. DON'T include an end time.

As mentioned in the previous chapter, dinner parties have no set end time. Furthermore, according to our friends (and regular guests) Lizzie Post and Daniel Post Senning—professional etiquette experts who are actual descendants of Emily Post herself—including an end time on a party invitation indicates to guests that they're welcome to show up *at any time* during the time range indicated. THIS IS NOT THE CASE AT A DINNER PARTY. People showing up midway through a dinner party will find all the pasta eaten and most of the booze consumed. They will then be hungry, sober, and mad.

4. DON'T forget your phone number.

We're assuming you're smart enough to know you should include, like, the actual address where the party's happening. But also throw your phone number on the invite. Especially if your pad's in a remote valley where GPS barely works. Folks cannot enjoy your dinner party if they get lost trying to find your ranch, run out of gas, and die in the desert.

INVITE METHODS: THREE SCENARIOS

Now that you know what information to provide on your invite, it's time to pick a method with which to transmit it. In our heady electronic age, you can choose from many. The good news: They all work, kind of. The bad news: They all suck, kind of. But depending on how far in advance you're planning your party, some methods are more suitable than others.

Scenario One:

You are a super energetic, mildly anal-retentive super-planner type and are preparing for your dinner party weeks in advance.

Suggested Invite Method: Custom Paper Invitation

A custom paper invitation, sent by mail, is the classiest and most classic way to announce a dinner party. Sending one is the closest you will ever get to feeling like the Queen of England, requesting the presence of Sir Mick Jagger for a post-polo soiree at Buckingham Palace.

By way of example:

Rico Gagliano and Brendan Francis Newnam
invite you to an intimate supper gathering at
The Dinner Party Download Autumn Cottage
in
West Eastberkmonshire-on-Thames, U.K
on
Saturday the Juneteenth of Rocktober, 2018
Pterodactyl and tamale dinner to be served at 7:30 p.m.
RSVP using the enclosed SASE
(555) RAD-GABS
Please, no cupcakes

Upsides: Looks cool. Makes invited guests feel special and valued. Also makes them feel guilty for even *thinking* about declining an invitation that obviously cost a ton of cash.

Downsides: Costs a ton of cash. Designing and mailing can take ten to a hundred times as long as the actual party will last. Makes guests think they're expected to dress up and wear a powdered wig or something.

Alternative: Just pick up a few greeting cards from the drugstore down the street, handwrite the relevant details inside, and mail those suckers. Avoid cards with clowns, balloons, or cheesy photos of windswept mountains on them.

❊ ❊ ❊

"[As a kid] I felt somehow nostalgic for a period I never lived through, I guess... I think in my mind somewhere I imagine that golden age exists. And there's a few moments where you have that, you know? Either you'll be at a really glamorous dinner, or at someone's home with some creative, wonderful people, and you think, 'Oh man, this is what it must have been like.' But it's such a rare, rare thing now."

— SCARLETT JOHANSSON

❊ ❊ ❊

Scenario Two:

You are a typical person who realizes, one Sunday, that you have the following weekend free. Hey, maybe you should invite some people over for a dinner party then!

Suggested Invite Method: Email

When the U.S. Defense Department created email, they were probably unaware it would be used mainly to transmit ads for Viagra and send dinner party invitations. But that is the case, and for this we both salute and are sad for them. Anyway, email is a quick yet unobtrusive way to alert your friends to an impending party—and gives them some time to respond.

Upsides: Near instantaneous delivery. Sense of shared friendship and intimacy as all invitees are immediately put in communication with you and each other. Recipients will appreciate receiving an email that is not an ad for Viagra.

Downsides: Invite may go unnoticed in recipient's inbox amidst all the ads for Viagra. And that aforementioned sense of group intimacy can also somehow spark a sense of group *ownership*, leading guests to behave as though *they* are throwing a party that happens to be in your home.

By way of example:

Subject: Dinner Party Friday!
From: RnB@dinnerpartiesawwwyeah.org
To: 4to12friends@potentialguests.tv; barack@bananacreamking.us
Hi guys! You're invited to our dinner party this Friday, at the DPD Penthouse high atop the Empire State Building. 7:30 p.m. Dress casual. Please, no pets, Brendan is allergic to dander and Rico is allergic to loud noise. Barack, you're on banana cream pie duty. Please RSVP!
Ciao,
Brendan & Rico
(555) FUN-PRTY

❧ ❧ ❧

Subject: Re: Dinner Party Friday!
From: 4to12friends@potentialguests.tv
To: RnB@dinnerpartiesawwwyeah.org; barack@bananacreamking.us
Awesome! But I can't make it Friday. Does Thursday work for everyone? Say 8 p.m.? P.S.: I have to bring my Doberman because he's recovering from rabies. But he's very quiet, and allergic people love him once he stops biting!
Signed,
Annoying Potential Guest

Subject: Re: Re: Dinner Party Friday!

From: barack@bananacreamking.us

To: 4to12friends@potentialguests.tv; RnB@dinnerpartiesawwwyeah.org

Dudes, this sounds sweet, but Thursday night doesn't work for me 'cause I've got a standing date to watch *Murder, She Wrote* reruns with Bader Ginsburg. How's 5:30 Wednesday night sound? P.S.: It's great that dogs are welcome at the party. We'll bring ours!

Best,

The B-meister

Subject: Re: Re: Re: Dinner Party Friday!

From: 4to12friends@potentialguests.tv

To: barack@bananacreamking.us; RnB@dinnerpartiesawwwyeah.org

Next Wednesday at 5:30 p.m. it is, Barack! Can't wait to meet your dog. P.S.: Please don't bring a banana cream pie like you always do; our Doberman is lactose intolerant.

EXCITED,

Annoying Potential Guest

Alternative: Use Evite or another free online invitation service. All the speed of an email invite, plus RSVPs are tallied for you, and there is no opportunity for invitees to screw up your plans, as above. Beware, however, that for no extra charge, these services will also turn your invite into a giant billboard festooned with sponsored ads — perhaps not the best way to indicate your party will be a respite from corporate capitalism. But we'll give you a pass for convenience's sake.

Scenario Three:

You are an irrepressibly impulsive little imp, and anyway, your hot Saturday night date just canceled on you. Screw it: you're inviting people over for dinner right now!

Suggested Invite Method: Group Text

Group texting is a perfectly legitimate way to extend an invitation to a casual or spur-of-the-moment party. It is also the invite method of last resort for hosts with a lot of lazy friends who didn't RSVP to the invite you sent a week ago.

Upsides: Speediest and most direct way to invite guests to your party. *Only* way to invite millennials to your party.

Downside: Of all invite methods, this is the one most likely to accidentally destroy a friendship.

By way of example:

> RnB
> Dudes did you get the cards, emails and evites we sent about our dinner party tonite

> RQ
> Yeah, but I didn't respond coz I didnt feel like it

> MZ
> No I dont check email anymore

> PD
> LOL Evite? Is it 2005?

RnB
OK well we're having a party tonite, 7:45 pm. We're serving foie gras tacos!

RQ
Cool will b there!

MZ
Thats ducking awesome c u then

MZ
(I mean FUCKING awesome I hate autocorrect)

PD
Is Rudy Quatro coming? We had casual sex yesterday & don't want to hang with him coz he'll think I actually like him

RnB
I think you meant to send that message privately, plus Rudy's on this thread, dawg

PD
Oh duck

RQ
: |

Alternative: Just call everyone on the phone and tell them to come over. By way of reminder, a "phone call" is when you use your phone not to text or take photographs but to *dial a number and actually speak to another person.* We know: weird! Note: Don't be surprised if a guest sounds panicked when they answer—they probably assume someone has died, because why else would you call in this day and age?

PART 2: WHO TO INVITE

Now that you've chosen *how* to ask people over, the next obvious question might seem to be, *who* should you ask?

Our answer to that, of course, is, whoever you like. We're not the Kremlin; we don't have an enemies blacklist for you or something.

But we do suggest that a more germane and important question at this point in your party planning might be, what *combination* of people should you invite? And as we stated in our MANIFESTO, it's our view that the goal of all hosts should be to shoot for the *unlikeliest mix of people possible.*

We acknowledge that this flies in the face of mainstream wisdom, which views a dinner party as a place solely for cozy quietude and mellow, conflict-free good times. Nonsense! In this ever-compartmentalized world, it's too easy to avoid encountering opinions or lifestyles different than our own. That may be awesome for mating and blood pressure, but it's bad for life, democracy, and boredom avoidance. A dinner party is a fine arena for cozy mellowness *and* respectful conflict, often *in the same night.*

✦ ✦ ✦

"I don't have a very diverse or inclusive set of friends. I don't have dinner parties with people who have different viewpoints than me politically. And that's a problem. You know, as much as I can criticize the close-mindedness and the privilege of someone that stays in their glass house and doesn't know people of color, I don't know any conservatives. I don't know any Christian conservatives that I can sit down with and have a meaningful conversation."

— AVA DUVERNAY, OSCAR-NOMINATED DIRECTOR OF SELMA AND 13TH

✦ ✦ ✦

Our favorite episodes of our show are when the guest list reads like it was devised by a guy with a borderline personality disorder on an ayahuasca trip.[4] Like the time a single episode featured the born-again Christian bassist from Megadeth, plus beach read queen Jackie Collins (RIP) and astrophysicist Neil deGrasse Tyson. Who knows? Seat all those people around a table and they might kill each other. But it's more likely they'll bounce ideas off each other until they reach a glorious ideological mash-up that could solve climate change and bring peace to Syria. But we guarantee the latter scenario *won't* happen if you invite over twelve versions of the same person, and you all just sit around smiling gently.

---

4   Actually, senior producer Jackson Musker books many of our guests. He's a sweet and brilliant trivia genius, pie baker, and pickup basketball junkie whose dad directed *The Little Mermaid.* Seriously: look it up.

But vocation and belief system aren't the only filters through which to pass your guest list. You'll also want to consider the proper mix of basic personalities. In our years of inviting guests to a weekly audio dinner party, we have found that all humans fall into one of several archetypes, each ideally balanced and offset by an equal and opposite one. For your convenience, we list each archetypical "pair" below. Avoid inviting one without the other.

Note that one of these people is YOU.

PAIR ONE:

a. The Narcissist

We know more about narcissists than anyone in the world.[5]

We regularly interview celebrities who're used to being treated as though the universe revolves around them, so we know whereof we speak. What's more, we interviewed a guy who literally wrote the book on the subject: journalist Jeffrey Kluger, author of *The Narcissist Next Door*. He provided us with this object lesson in classic narcissism:

> There was a woman [I met] who was eighty-five years
> old. And she was talking about her past, and talked
> about how she got out of a bad marriage when her
> husband went to fight World War II.
>   And she said, "It makes me wonder if this war was
> really fought to defeat Hitler…or to get *me* out of a bad
> situation." And she said that shamelessly, and without
> self-awareness.

Ah yes, who could forget FDR's classic declaration of war?: "Yesterday, December seventh, nineteen forty-one—a date which will live in infamy—the United States of America entered the deadliest international conflict of all time, in order to end this one random woman's lousy marriage."

Our takeaway here is that narcissists are everywhere. They come in all forms, from eighty-five-year-old war widows, to show-off baristas, to United States presidents.

And yet narcissists make wonderful dinner party guests! They're often charming, they can be great to look at, they've got endless reams of undeniably interesting stories about themselves, and at the very least their total self-absorption can be fascinating to witness. But beware: Like saffron and Adele songs, a little goes a long way. The same narcissist whose ego can bring a blast of energy to a gathering can also steamroll conversation. They're good to have around in case of a fire, because they can suck all the oxygen out of a room.

BALANCE WITH:

b. The Subtle Undercutter

The Subtle Undercutter is the most quiet and innocuous-seeming person at the party. Indeed, other guests might initially wonder why you invited such a mouse to your shindig. Then the Narcissist says something boastful, outrageous, or otherwise lame, and the Subtle Undercutter chimes in with a single phrase that deftly puts the offender in their place. Everyone laughs—including the skewered narcissist, because what else is there to do? The Subtle Undercutter has been so quiet and nice that there is no barb to hurl back! It's kind of a magical thing.

It can be hard to know who amongst your friends, family, or acquaintances is a Subtle Undercutter, on account of them being, you know, subtle. It's only in a party situation that their true nature blooms forth. But we've seen elderly Midwestern women, after decades of putting up with mildly racist blowhard husbands, become adept Subtle Undercutters. Have a glass or two of sherry on hand to rev them up.

PAIR TWO:

a. The Name-Dropper

Allow us to describe the Name-Dropper by dropping a name: former prince of talk shows Dick Cavett. He's one of our favorite recurring guests, and would be near the top of any rational person's dream party guest list — despite the fact that a transcript of a conversation with him reads like the hotel registry at the Chateau Marmont. In his four visits to our show, he's managed to "casually" mention encounters with Groucho Marx, Katharine Hepburn, Alfred Hitchcock, Gore Vidal, George H. W. Bush, Spiro Agnew, and John Lennon.

"Groucho left a party once early, in Los Angeles, with a rather snooty hostess who said, 'Leaving, Mr. Marx?' And Groucho said, 'I've had a wonderful evening — but this wasn't it.'"
— DICK CAVETT

۷

Cavett is the best sort of name-dropper: Each name he drops is in service to a great anecdote; the celebrities mentioned are of such cultural importance that the mere utterance of their names adds class to the proceedings; and hearing his tales about them evokes our common story. For better or worse, celebrities are this era's Greek gods, playing out our fears and fantasies at a safe distance.

ENDAN FRANCIS NEWNAM

RICO GAGLIANO

62

Unfortunately, most name-droppers aren't Dick Cavett. They brag about celebrity sightings to bolster their low self-esteem, adding nothing to your party but a sense of pathos. Many of these name-droppers host public radio culture shows.

BALANCE WITH:

b. The Sleeper

The Sleeper is the guest who's so money, she doesn't know she's money. The hidden gem who other guests discover lurking in their midst like a rare baby panda. In a manner similar to that of the Subtle Undercutter, the Sleeper is quiet at first. But over the course of the evening, as conversation and wine flow, this person slowly, humbly reveals that they are in fact the most interesting individual at the table. The Name-Dropper's glamorous tales suddenly pale in comparison to this real live human being sitting before you.

The Sleeper is rarely a celebrity. Most often they're a scientist working in some obscure corner of an obscure field, the world-shaking importance of which they're able to easily convey to your increasingly delighted guests. Or perhaps they're a retiree who, they eventually admit with a hint of embarrassment, once spent two years on a commune with Leonard Cohen. The Sleeper is a regular, relatable person whose name one would never drop, but who does or has done stuff you can't imagine.

The "Chattering Class" section of our show is basically a weekly repository for Sleepers: the mild author who spent years visiting every potential site of the legendary lost city of Atlantis, the perennial TV extra who specialized in playing corpses. They're some of our favorite guests.

But be warned: Occasionally the Sleeper is "asleep" for good reason—i.e., they turn out to be fucking nuts. Keep a cell phone and a spanner handy in case one of the fascinating things the Sleeper reveals is that they were a mob assassin, and that they kind of miss it.

a. The Eeyore

Also known to baby boomers as the "Debbie Downer" and to millennials as the "Emo Kid," the Eeyore is a misanthrope. A grump. A bummer. In short, a realist who refuses to pretend that life is anything more than an endless parade of mean people beating up Mother Nature until she buries us with earthquakes and tsunamis.

Sounds like just the dude you want at your party, right? But like narcotics, if deployed sparingly, an Eeyore can actually *heighten* the effects of a good gathering. We need a little tension and conflict to be entertained. And Eeyores can be counted upon to provide both, because they disagree with everything. Note these two possible conversational scenarios.

Scenario 1

> YOU: I love cute puppies!

> GUEST: Me too! Here is a picture of mine.

Scenario 2

> YOU: I love cute puppies!

> EEYORE: They grow up to either bite us, or die and leave
> us grieving.

Scenario 2 forces you to examine the nature of pet ownership, to defend your emotional attachment to an animal whose true thoughts and motives remain largely unknown even to science, and to perhaps dig into the Eeyore's background to try and learn what rendered them immune to the obvious awesome cuteness of baby mammals with large watery eyes and sweet, clumsy little legs. Whereas scenario 1 can only lead to a half hour of you and your guest calling up ever-cuter puppy pictures from the depths of your cell phones. We know which interaction would leave *us* feeling enriched.

That said, too much Eeyore can obviously turn a party into a suicide watch. In fact, a recent survey showed that 85 percent of party fouls were committed by unremittingly bleak Eeyores.

BALANCE WITH:

b. The Comedian

Comedians have a twinkle in their eye, an infectious laugh, no fear of strangers, and a commitment to making people chuckle. A Comedian is genetically compelled to force an Eeyore to crack a smile, or at least force the Eeyore to acknowledge the ridiculousness of his/her implacable grumpitude.

All good things. Yet hanging out with a Comedian can be a bit like sticking your head out the window of a moving car. It feels good for a while, until your face, mouth, and ears start to feel like pulled taffy. Constant hilarity is exhausting, but the Comedian lives to laugh and get laughs. They have zero sense of when enough is enough.

Another drawback: The Comedian thinks everything is fair game for a punch line, including religion, terrorism, and other guests' sincere tales of personal tragedy. We support ribald humor and mischief (see chapter six), but the goal is to create an atmosphere wherein guests can say anything— and the Comedian's irreverence can have a chilling effect.

The key moments at which to activate Comedians, then, are the beginning and end of the evening, when it's good to have someone with no boundaries break the ice or rev up others' flagging energy.[6] But work on keeping them subdued during the middle portion of the evening, when

---

6   There's a reason comedians are used on sitcom sets to keep the live audience engaged during three solid hours of hearing the same lame jokes over and over.

richer conversations traditionally flourish. Suggestion: Prepare a meal you know they'll love. It's hard to talk with your mouth full. Although they'll try.

Also keep an eye on Comedians' alcohol consumption. They will invariably tend toward having one too many, at which point they will reveal themselves to be, at heart, Eeyores.

PAIR FOUR:

a. The Single and Proud

Technically, Single and Prouds aren't guests — they've just come to grab food between dates. Dates with boys. Dates with girls. Dates with start-up companies. Doesn't matter. They want…they take. At least that's what they *say*. In reality, who knows? Single and Prouds send a lot of mixed messages. On the one hand, a recent hookup is described disdainfully as "the reason abortion should remain legal," and yet same said hookup would "make a great parent" and is the Single and Proud's date to an upcoming wedding. One moment the Single and Proud expounds on the joys of being answerable to no one; the next they're stabbing their hand with a fork while a couple talks about their recent adorable trip to Tulum.

The Single and Proud's titillating stories of romantic conquests can often veer into overshare territory, especially if they're seated near established couples. They'll say things like, "Oh — you guys have a joint bank account?! That's cute. *I* have joint custody of a submissive named Mars."

A Single and Proud can add a nice jolt to a dinner party. Just keep them away from couples on the rocks.

BALANCE WITH:

b. The Hipster

You can smell them before they arrive: the rich scent of cedar and cold-press coffee excreted through the ink of tattooed pores. A hybrid of yuppie and store-bought bohemian. The Navy SEALs of gentrification. The Hipsters.

Whereas the Single and Proud is needy and provocative, the Hipster teems with party confidence. They are "up" on every single thing of cultural importance, plus the stuff that's *going to* be of cultural importance in the future. Therefore, the Hipster loves dinner parties—one of the few arenas outside arts journalism where all this knowledge is of any value. Hungry after a long day of being ironic, they'll arrive fashionably (how else?) late and happily request an obscure cocktail you don't have ingredients for, jam your conversational radar with an obscure pop reference, and then inhale your meal using nothing but their phone's camera.

While potentially vapid and sad in the long term, over the brief course of a dinner party the Hipster provides delightful and essential conversational currency. We also recommend deploying social jujitsu to turn their exacting, curatorial tastes to the party's advantage. A good tactic: Install them behind the bar. (Hipsters are natural mixologists: as children they whipped up Juicy Juice Manhattans and chocolate milk martinis.) Or ask them to DJ. (After they've publicly condemned your record collection, you can count on them to conjure solid grooves out of their Pono,[7] not one of which you will have ever heard before.)

The Hipster will also happily talk up—and likely leave with—the Single and Proud. They collect interesting dates, as they do everything else.

PAIR FIVE:

a. The Eager Beaver

Amazing but true: Some people actually *like* to help and do stuff. These are the Eager Beavers. The Cuisinart of dinner party guests, the Eager Beaver minces, chops, blends, and is really hard to put back together once

---

7   What, you don't know what that is?

taken apart. So put them to work! Shelling walnuts, washing mushrooms, setting the table, preparing your taxes—you name it. The Eager Beaver is your essential backup: your Alfred the butler, your Flavor Flav, your best friend who can vouch that on the night of the murder,[8] the two of you were hanging out at her place.

The trick with Eager Beavers is making sure they don't end up taking over your event. Stand firm when they try to make your olives "better" by stuffing them with mayo. Resist when they offer to answer the door for you. Stop them when they attempt to spank your children for eating all the Goldfish crackers or start making up endearing nicknames for your spouse. Deep down, the Eager Beaver is uncomfortable being a guest; don't let them become the host.

BALANCE WITH:

b. The Bad Drunk

This is, you know, a bad drunk. For the host, the Bad Drunk is an embarrassing tragedy. But you might want to invite one for the benefit of the Eager Beaver, for whom the Bad Drunk is a wonderfully all-consuming nightlong *project*.

A NOTE TO GUESTS

Congratulations! You have been invited to a dinner party via one of the methods described herein. Now what?

RULE #1: RSVP

We understand you're busy. But a dinner party invitation indicates that someone finds you interesting enough to want to spend a semi-

---

8   Wait a minute. Where were *you*?

intimate evening with. They're also offering to feed you. At least tell them whether you're going to show up! And do it quickly—particularly if you can't make it. Remember: If your host is using this book properly, they have identified your archetypal personality and have invited another guest with an offsetting personality for balance. If you flake, the host will need as much time as possible to find another narcissist to take your place.

RULE #2: THOU SHALT NOT ADDITIONALLY INVITE

Dinner parties are not frat keggers or holiday parties, where the host's *goal* is to have so many people show up that she doesn't know who half of them are. A host puts actual thought into a dinner party guest list and may only be able to physically accommodate a certain number of people. So if you're invited to a dinner party, assume you're the only one invited — don't bring someone along without asking the host if it's cool. However, NOTE TO HOSTS: If you invite a guest who's part of a couple, expect the other half of the couple to show up. Especially if you are the guest's ex.

RULE #3: NOW IS THE TIME FOR THE DIETARY-RESTRICTIONS CONVERSATION

You are a lactose intolerant vegan celiac. You would like not to be restricted to eating only carrot sticks at your host's party. Fair enough. What you do is, *immediately upon RSVP'ing,* ask if it's okay to bring an all-plant lactose-and-gluten-free entrée for yourself. Your host will very likely tell you not to bother, because they've got your dietary needs covered...or they'll delightedly welcome your offer.

The time to bring up your dietary restriction is specifically *not* when you show up at the party. At that point, your job is to happily eat the carrot sticks.

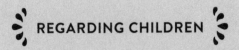

REGARDING CHILDREN

For whom is a dinner party recess? *Adults.* Who are not adults? *Children.*

An overabundance of little ones underfoot will negate everything that makes a dinner party a dinner party. You cannot be spontaneous and freewheeling in an environment where you're not allowed to utter a four-letter word, lest you sully a child's tender ears. It is exponentially more difficult to bond with peers over conversations of substance (or even silliness) if you have to pause every five seconds to pry the fondue fork out of little Olivia's hand before she stabs the cat. You cannot take a break from the pressures of adulthood while a child — the physical manifestation of adulthood's most awesome responsibility — is all up in your grill.

We love kids, though, and are in favor of *exposing* them to dinner parties, thus enculturating them early to the pleasures of the form. We ourselves fondly remember our own parents' dinner gatherings, during which we got to spend the evening in the TV room watching *Battlestar Galactica* while, in the dining room, the grown-ups' laughter kept getting louder and louder for some reason.

And that is the key: If some guests want to bring their kids, that's fine, as long as the kids can be sequestered *away from the dinner party.*[9]

Obviously, this means that the children need to be mature enough to, like, go to the bathroom on their own, and entertain themselves without setting fire to the curtains or each other. Also, you'll need a place big enough that you can only hear the children if they're screaming in pain. Therefore, alas, efficiency dwellers: your guests will just have to hire a babysitter.

Of course, you can have a swell time welcoming parents with younger infants and toddlers into your home! Just be aware that when you do, you are having a baby playdate, not a dinner party.

---

9   Sleeping babies exempted.

✦ ✦ ✦

"My [journalist] parents had some of the best dinner parties [in Washington, DC]...I used to climb under the dining room table with a pillow, thinking that none of them knew I was there. Like, I would army crawl under their legs, and just lay down and listen to them talk...And at one point Mick Jagger was there...and he just said, 'Go to bed!'"

— OLIVIA WILDE

✦ ✦ ✦

CHAPTER THREE

BEFORE THE SHOW

You are now fully committed. People are going to come over and be in your home and eat your food. It is at this moment that the amateur dinner party host hyperventilates, sucks down a bunch of Zolofts, and tries to convince an Uber driver to return them to their mother's womb.

After all, there are hors d'oeuvres to prepare. Hours of music to be selected. You are suddenly certain your entire home must be thoroughly cleaned, and every crevice bombed with antibacterial agents. Maybe you should go to Bed Bath & Beyond and invest in a bushel of potpourri. You will need to hire an expensive DJ and caterers—that's for sure. While you're at it, you better also order a tablecloth made of pinktoe tarantula spider silk. Perhaps you should have the house remodeled for the occasion? Yes, who could possibly enjoy themselves in your stupid old house, which does not have an open floor plan? *You better knock out half the walls in your house to create an open floor plan or you will be derided as a failure!!*

Reader, relax. Do not remodel your home. As we mentioned in the previous chapter, unless your last name is Windsor, people aren't coming to your party expecting to dine in sumptuous luxury. Remember our MANIFESTO: *Perfect imperfection!* Humans are not perfect, nor are our homes.

This is a party, not a photo shoot for a Swedish travel brochure. This is recess for adults. And like a recess playground, all that's really necessary is a space conducive to social interaction, where no one's going to accidentally split their head open.

* ↑ *

"I hate parties, so I wouldn't invite anyone over. But if I had to, I'd invite way more people than I could fit into the apartment, because that would make everybody really grouchy. I like that."

— Oscar the Grouch (a.k.a. puppeteer Caroll Spinney)

* ↑ *

Creating such a space does require a modicum of effort, though. And thus the precious few days or hours between sending out your party invites and hooking your guests up to a Pinot Noir IV are critical — though not necessarily expensive or difficult. Read this chapter and we guarantee you dinner party satori. Herein we will help you prepare your party's a) physical setting, b) music, and c) appetizers. In the process, we will also attempt to make you chuckle four to ten times.

PART 1: SETTING THE SCENE

You are a busy person. Your home is in some state of disorganization. Perhaps you skipped spring cleaning this year. Or for the last several years. To really whip the joint into shape would probably require a janitorial staff, armed with a pressure washer full of toxic cleansers.

Once again, *you don't have to whip the joint into that kind of shape.* Let us take you step by step through the minimum amount of toil necessary to create a dinner party–ready physical environment.

Note: These steps are listed in order of importance. The only *essential* one is the first. Anything after that is gravy.

STEP 1: BATHROOM

Let's say you take a mystery psychadelic the night before your dinner party and wake up, sans kidney, beneath a pile of strippers on an unmoored boat in the Ohio River. You finally stumble back into your house with five minutes to spare before guests arrive. What should be *the first thing* you do?

Destroy your cell phone. But after that? Clean your bathroom.

Every other facet of dinner partying can be faked to some extent.[1] If all goes absolutely wrong, you can always buy prepared foods to go, you can serve canned beer, you can even use Tinder to find yourself some guests. But you can't fake a clean bathroom.

Bathrooms are the teeth of your home; they must be maintained not just for the sake of health and hygiene, but because they're so awful to see in a state of decay. This is the one room in your place in which every guest will spend time alone, probably with a bright overhead light illuminating every corner and surface.

So clean your bathroom and clean it well. If you're the type of person who thinks it's totally fine to leave a frosting of shaving cream mottled with stubble on your sink basin and a wet Target circular on the floor next to your toilet, then we suggest you cancel your dinner party, and instead strip to your tighty-whities and cozy up with a TV dinner in your sty, as is likely your custom and preference.

> PRO TIP: Take a peek inside your medicine cabinet — your guests will! Best to relocate questionable pills to your hall closet and/or gullet.

---

1   Our publisher's marketing department asked us not to say that, but it's true, and anyway we seriously doubt they've read this far.

STEP 2: DINING ROOM

The dining room is the main stage of the night. If you've cleaned the bathroom and have any time remaining, try making sure the dining room has good lighting and is free of clutter.

Note: By "good" lighting we do *not* mean "bright" lighting. Indeed, "good" lighting, in a dinner party context, means your dining area would ideally be more Vermeer than interrogation room. To achieve the right effect, deploy candles. Also lampshades.[2] Dim light is magic. It makes wrinkles disappear and it makes spills undetectable. It's like applying a Valencia Instagram filter to everything.

As for clutter, the dining room is a landing pad for food and increasingly tipsy guests. So you might want to remove obstacles that could cause either to fall to the floor. Like the shoes you hurriedly kicked off as you raced into the house to clean up before the party.

Remove keys, piles of mail, and bike parts from the dinner table, lest you try to set a gravy boat atop them and thereby liberally sauce your tablecloth.

If you've got a sideboard, it can hold extra napkins, bottles of wine, or art framed under protective glass. But you might want to clear away the vintage Spider-Man issue number one you wanted to show off later in the evening, unless you're eager for someone to leave a circular wineglass stain on your kid's future college tuition.

> PRO TIP: Flowers make a great centerpiece...*before* dinner. Once food is on the table, move them to a side table or another room. Flowers not only give off scents that can conflict with food and/or induce allergies; they block sight lines across the table and make everyone feel like they're talking to plants, which worked out for Moses but will drive your guests insane.

---

2   These can double for headgear later.

STEP 3: LIVING ROOM

More likely than not, a dinner party will begin and end in the living room. This is where cocktails are served at the start of the night, and where they're spilled at the end.

There's only one thing you *must* do when tidying your living room, and that's shut off the goddamn television and hide the remotes. As mentioned in chapter one, TVs are a dinner party's Professor Moriarty, Lex Luthor, and Lord Voldemort combined. They are conversation destroyers and portals into everything a dinner party guest is meant to escape: strangers' agendas, impersonal entertainment, commercials for adult diapers.

Once the TV is defused, should you have the time, feel free to do the basics: run a vacuum, fluff a pillow, extract any wadded-up paper napkin wontons from between your couch cushions.

Next, maybe take a look at your bookshelves: do those books have the potential to inspire conversation? Seriously: *Penny Stocks for Dummies? Quicken 3 User's Manual? Fast 'n' Easy Miracle Whip Cookbook? Fodor's Malta 2005?*[3] Think about moving these and similar titles to another room, to the bottom shelf, or hey: why not the recycling bin? Throwing a party is a great excuse to purge your home of chaff. Trust us: you won't miss last year's Boxes Unlimited catalog.

> PRO TIP: Your living room coffee table is an ideal place to leave a conversation piece: a book on a subject you'd like to chat about, a souvenir from an interesting journey you've been on, or an item removed from your body through surgery.

---

3   A 1950s Fodor's is neat, and a current Fodor's means you just went, or are going, to Malta. But one from ten years back is kind of like proudly showing off an unwashed dish — a soiled and useless remnant of a good time had by others long ago.

STEP 4: KITCHEN

Years ago, in one of those *New York Times* Style pieces disguised as journalism, the "Caligula" look was proclaimed to be "in." Caligula—as the liberal arts majors and/or *Penthouse* magazine readers among you may recall—was the unhinged Roman ruler who had a taste for parties, murders, and messes. And according to this article, the new cool thing to do was leave your house in disarray: dirty dishes on the coffee table, soiled glasses on the nightstand, full ashtrays...you get the picture.

Like most Style pieces,[4] the story was utter horse hockey created on a dare by a tipsy writer who made up the headline first and then quoted a bunch of pals to "confirm the trend." As we hope we're making clear in this chapter, you at least want to *attempt* some amount of tidiness before company arrives.

There *is* one room, however, where the Caligula look is not only acceptable but desirable: the kitchen. Olive oil bottles without tops, a colander resting on a coffee mug, flour fingerprints on the cabinets—all great. A sloppy kitchen means good things are afoot. Opened tins and popped bottles create an air of abundance and industry that will contribute to the warmth that is a key ingredient of a dinner party. Here you can be a mad wizard stirring a pot with one hand, cranking the lettuce spinner with the other, phone wedged under your ear, drinking wine through a long straw and shaking your hips to a Missy Elliott number.

In other words, to prep your kitchen for a dinner party, spill something in there.

STEP 5: BEDROOM

Bedrooms are like the secret thoughts nestled deep in the darkest regions of your heart: you don't necessarily want to share them with everybody. So it's

---

4   Except the one we used to partly justify this entire book in the prologue.

perfectly legit to make your boudoir off-limits to guests. The universal code to indicate this: Shut the door to your room. Boom, you're done.[5]

But maybe you *want* to show off your bedroom. Or maybe you want to go the classic route and use your bed as a repository for guests' coats. This is not only practical (we have yet to find a coatrack that can handle twelve winter jackets) but creates an excellent wool, fur, and pleather pile into which your guests' kids can burrow.

If this is how you want to roll, do a commonsense sweep of the space: make your bed, hide any marital aids. Actually, you may want to do this anyway, just in case: at modern dinner parties, bedrooms often serve as discreet cell phone booths into which guests sneak, in order to check in on babysitters, basketball game scores, or mistresses.

> PRO TIP: Leave only a bedside reading lamp illuminated. This will provide sufficient light to prevent people from face-planting into a bedpost while keeping the room dim enough to prevent them from stumbling upon your zipper-mouth fetish mask collection.

STEP 6: STOP

If you've made it this far, you've cleaned and arranged far more than necessary and are probably the kind of person who will now compulsively start arranging your socks in alphabetical order by color. Stop, for God's sake— you've got music and hors d'oeuvres to prepare. And take heart: after the party, you get to clean up everything all over again! With a hangover (see chapter seven).

---

5   To reinforce the "Keep out" concept, kill all overhead hallway lights in the back of your home so that the only illumination is coming from the open bathroom. One cannot snoop in a bedroom one cannot find.

PART 2: PREPARING THE MUSIC

A musicless party is like food without salt: serviceable but dull. Music provides the background energy that makes a dinner party feel less "dinner" and more "party." Music can trigger nostalgic reveries in your guests or inspire political debate. It can also smooth over any inevitable quiet lulls in conversation, or fill in the astonished silence after the Comedian makes a crude joke about another guest's disintegrating marriage. Just about the only thing music can't improve at a party is stale bread. And music can conceivably do that, too, if it gets everyone dancing so hard that the room becomes shrouded with a humidifying fog of sweat.

As the German philosopher Friedrich Nietzsche said, "Without music, life would be a mistake."[6]

That said, the wrong music, played at the wrong time, via the wrong music system, can also kill a party. Luckily, we are full of insight regarding the preparation and execution of great party music.

STEP 1: CHOOSE YOUR WEAPON

Below are the three party-friendliest technological methods for playing music, in what we believe to be ascending order of excellence.

3. Classical, Jazz, or College Radio

You may have neither the time nor the inclination to amass a personal music collection. Or you may earn a meager income you must spend on, like, food and utility bills, rather than on music and equipment through which to play it. For you, there is gloriously free broadcast radio.

Alas, we cannot recommend that you tune in most commercial radio

---

6   He also said "God is Dead"—a clear reference to his love for a certain pioneering California jam band.

stations because, um, *the word "commercial" is right in their name.* Indeed, for every one song played, you will hear three billionmillion commercials. Remember what we said about not befouling your dinner table with corporate packaging? Same rule applies to your guests' ears.

Luckily, most jazz and classical stations are ad-free. The song selections—and even the DJs' soothing, oboe-like voices—make fine background music. Only potential risk: the occasional random appearance of Mannheim Steamroller.

If you're in the mood for something louder, tune in your local "alternative rock" college station. Another fine, commercial-free choice—assuming you've done your research and know tonight's DJ isn't going to follow every song with a half hour of impenetrable inside jokes about her dorm mates.

2. Turntable (a.k.a. Phonograph, Record Player, Turny Thing Which Plays Those Huge Black CDs)

Yes, we know, vinyl record collecting has become an expensive[7] and insufferable hobby for rich hipsters. But that's one of the appeals of picking a turntable as your musical method of choice: neutralizing the scorn of any rich hipsters you may have invited. Indeed, play your cards just right and they may spend the entire evening thumbing through your records and providing you with free DJ services.[8]

More importantly (and practically), though, turntables are the ideal tool for pacing a dinner party. This is because, like fires, they must be

---

7   For a *cheap* party-friendly vinyl starter set, take five bucks to Goodwill and get the following for a dollar each: Herb Alpert and the Tijuana Brass's *Whipped Cream and Other Delights,* Tracy Chapman's *Tracy Chapman,* ELO's *A New World Record,* Michael Jackson's *Thriller,* and anything by Nat King Cole. Trust us: they'll all be there.

8   To *guarantee* this happens, sprinkle your collection liberally with deluxe reissues of obscure albums from the record labels Light in the Attic and 4 Men with Beards.

constantly tended. Every twenty minutes or so—the average running time of a vinyl side—you will be given an opportunity to recalibrate the mood of the evening. Is everyone getting a little too worked up about the president's latest tweet? Oops, that Iron Maiden record just ended; time for some show tunes! Okay, now what were we discussing again? Something about the theater, wasn't it?

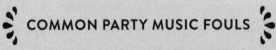

COMMON PARTY MUSIC FOULS

THE MULTIPLE-FORMAT MISTAKE

Pick a format and stick to it for at least an hour at a time. Constantly skipping from record player to CD player to digital streaming can result in songs being halted midplay—ruining the vibe and, possibly, conversation.

MUSICAL COMMUNALISM

The ideal dinner party is a musical dictatorship. That musical dictator is YOU, unless you bequeath this power to ONE guest of your choosing. Be vigilant! Otherwise you'll find your stereo hijacked over and over by guests who insist that everybody just *has to hear* this *one song*. It will never be just one song. It will always be several songs. And your guests will not be selecting them for the good of the party—they will be selecting them for *themselves*.

THE TELEVISION TRAP

If your music setup requires you to select or play tunes through your TV monitor, *figure out a different setup*. A TV set displaying a playlist and album art is as distracting as anything else on a TV. Plus, you've introduced the temptation to use the TV set to play video. At which point your party is fucked.

1. Homemade Digital Playlist Played via Any Means Necessary

We can't state it enough: The key difference between dinner parties and the Day-Killing Egg Meal That Shall Not Be Named is *your personal touch*. Just as the food you serve reflects your personality, so does the music you play. So while the above musical methods are totally serviceable (and take way less time to prep), the most accurate way to musically represent yourself is to compile a playlist of your favorite songs. Plus, unlike a vinyl record, a playlist can be hours and hours long. And unlike a radio DJ's set, a homemade soufflé, or your friend Ali's endless stories about her kid, a playlist is always perfect. Because it came from you.

STEP 2: PREPARING YOUR PLAYLIST

Some of our best friends are musicians, but even they'll tell you musicians often make for lousy interviews.[9] Maybe because they're exhausted from touring. Maybe because they can't hear our questions, after spending years battered by tidal waves of guitar distortion. Most likely it's because answering questions with earnest insight doesn't tend to boost your rock star cred. In any case, to combat the problem, we created a segment called the Dinner Party Soundtrack. Wherein we ask musicians to list a few tunes they'd play at a party. Because even if they won't deign to explain why they rhymed "Girl I love you" with "Squirrels gonna mug you," they're usually psyched to talk about a few songs they've been digging.

Anyway, a happy side benefit of putting this part of the show together

---

9 Among the exceptions: most veteran musicians over fifty years of age. Elvis Costello readily admitted to us that as a young punk, the moment a journalist approached him, "that's when [I] put on the act"—i.e., he became a surly monosyllabic jerk. Whereas in his sixties, as he is now, he was happy to regale us with tales about the time he taped a TV lemonade jingle with his dad, or the time Joe Strummer tried on his glasses.

has been learning, over time, that for most people, dinner parties unfold in three distinct phases, each demanding a certain vibe of music. Structure your playlist with these phases in mind — about forty-five minutes' worth of songs each — and you'll be the boss of bossa nova, the soul of soul, the… unk of funk? Whatever. You'll be golden.

Phase One: The Welcome

Everyone's arriving. Hugs, handshakes, and/or air-kisses. Guests who've never met greet each other with delighted, squeaky-high voices, as they wait for the first glass of booze to take effect and make socializing way easier.

Our own rule of thumb is to score this phase of the party with music that's upbeat and not too wordy, to facilitate conversation and sweeten the sound of glasses clinking. Our guests don't always agree.

"Distant Lover" — Marvin Gaye

"It's a pretty sexy song. I think that would be a nice mood-setting song. Y'know, people walking in the door are like, 'Aaaall right! It's gonna be this kinda party.'"

— KEVIN BARNES, OF MONTREAL

"Cold Turkey" — John Lennon

"When we first get to this party, the song that's going to be playing is 'Cold Turkey' by John Lennon. I chose this track to be a little witty — add a little food humor to the mix. And then also I want to keep my guests educated on the perils of food storage. The typical interpretation of this song is that it's about heroin withdrawal, but I've heard that it is actually inspired by a time when John Lennon got food poisoning from actual cold turkey, and he intentionally wrote it so that it could be interpreted as heroin withdrawal instead."

— WILL TOLEDO, A.K.A. CAR SEAT HEADREST

"No Sleep till Brooklyn" — *The Beastie Boys*

"I've been living in Brooklyn for nearly twenty years now. It's definitely home at this point. So, the first song of my dinner party will be 'No Sleep till Brooklyn.' I mean, just the hook — who comes up with that, you know what I mean? And the way they yell it at you: 'BROOKLYYYYN!'"

— SANTIGOLD

"Rumble" — *Link Wray*

"It just has this sort of really menacing feel to it, like something stormy just walked through the door."

— DANIEL KESSLER, INTERPOL

"Island Ridin'" — *The So So Glos*

"I wanna get the guests pumped at this party. So we're gonna start on an upbeat note while all the finger foods are getting passed around. Maybe some people will even dance, you know? With those crab rolls in their hands."

— CONOR OBERST

Phase Two: Dinner

With some cocktails in their veins, everyone is now best friends, and you all sit down to dinner. We figure this is the perfect time to drop in a song that might *itself* become the subject of dinner conversation (see blues rocker Benjamin Booker's pick, below). But a lot of musicians have told us this might also be an appropriate time for screaming high-octane rock. We figure that's because they're used to eating dinner in their dressing room while an opening act sound-checks just down the hall at stun volume. But maybe that's how you want to feel, too.

"Long Tall Sally" — *Little Richard*

"I'm hoping that by now, especially if it's winter, we would be having some Chianti Classico... and so I think I would go with 'Long Tall Sally' by Little Richard. I mean, Chianti Classico — you gotta get the right one — it's a lovely light Italian wine, and it's something you can drink in quite large quantities. And I would like to feel everyone's feeling fairly loose and ready for a good ol' knees-up."

— COLIN BLUNSTONE, THE ZOMBIES

"New Noise" — Refused

"So now, at this point [in the party], everyone's turnt up…It's just raucous, everyone's just bouncing off each other. It's almost like when you're at a rally and everyone's together, in unison, saying the same thing. That kind of energy. But it's a fun energy."

— DJ STEVE AOKI

"Smooth" — Santana feat. Rob Thomas

"Everyone knows it, and, really, everyone loves it. I think it's kind of an icebreaker, where someone hears it playing and they go, Oh! 'Smooth'! And then people sing along or just start talking about it…Also, my name in Japanese means 'ocean moon,' and there's a line in that song that says, 'Just like the ocean under the moon.' So I was like, 'Oh my God, that's me! That's me!'"

— MITSKI

"Brazil" — Les Paul

"I imagine this song being around a salad course at a dinner party. What makes me think of a salad course is there's these crazy little really high-pitched kind of guitar 'stabs' in this song. It reminds me of when you're eating a salad, you've got a fork, and you're stabbing at a little renegade cherry tomato all over the plate and can't get it."

— NICK KRILL, THE SPINTO BAND

"So What"—*Miles Davis*

"I love eating to jazz. There's just something about it. It's deep and rich.
"And it's very, very good for the digestive system. Your organs are like a musical band. And when you've got the combination of good company, good music, and good food... ohhh, that band can play.
"I've heard this song my entire life. It's been places. It's shot heroin. It's failed. But then it recovered. It's kind of like a survivor. Which is something I can relate to."

— Xavier Dphrepaulezz, a.k.a. Fantastic Negrito

"Any Other Way"—*Jackie Shane*

"It's good background music, you know: soft, but also entertaining. People might stop eating for a second and be like, 'Oh, what is this?' And I'll be like, 'Oh, it's Jackie Shane.'
"Jackie Shane is an R & B singer from Toronto, who used to wear women's clothing and dress up. Like, this black soul singer cross-dressing guy. And it's the most incredible stuff that you've ever heard. I don't think people know very much about this guy, and that's what makes it so crazy. It's like, what was happening in Toronto that you have this guy who's doing stuff that's completely taboo, in the early sixties? Where does he come from? I don't know—you tell me. You tell me!"

— Benjamin Booker

Phase Three: Dancing/Lounging

Dinner done, the evening can conclude in one of two ways: with a bang or with a (contented food coma) whimper. In the case of the former, you need music that can fuel dancing, increasingly hysterical laughter, or the sound of your bookcase collapsing 'cause your tipsy friend stumbled into it. In the case of the latter, you seek music that might lead your guests to fall happily asleep midsentence. Either way, apparently, it is the ideal time to play David Bowie.

CORIN TUCKER, SLEATER-KINNEY

"Changes"—David Bowie

"I was thinking, you know, maybe the food is done, maybe we're going to move to a different room. So I think that having this song, 'Changes,' would actually provide a good segue into a change: change of scene for the party."

— CORIN TUCKER, SLEATER-KINNEY

"Magic Dance"—David Bowie, from the Labyrinth *soundtrack*

"'Magic Dance' is the weirdest song ever made by anyone that's ever made music. You see who knows this song. You judge 'em off of that. If they don't know it, and they've never seen Labyrinth, you're probably not inviting them [to a party] next year. You put it on, you get a Soul Train line going."

— MACKLEMORE

"Crazy"—Seal

"It's mellow enough to where, if you guys want to two-step and shake your shoulders to it? That's cool. If you also want to run and jump through your neighbor's windowpane naked? Totally goes with both of those."

— THUNDERCAT

"I Have Walked This Body"—Susanna and Jenny Hval

"The first line is, 'I have walked this body to the rim of its end.' It sounds like somebody maxing out their body until they physically just leave it. If I was having a dinner party...eventually I would want to get real occulty, you know what I mean? Like, we're all there around a table; we

might as well do some kind of ritual, or have some kind of
out-of-body experience."
— MIKE HADREAS, A.K.A. PERFUME GENIUS

"Guilty"—Al Bowlly, 1930s jazz singer

"Al has this way of crooning — this high tenor that lilts
and floats... It blends in well, you can mingle and talk...
And for whatever reason, it's a very warm and welcoming
sound, hearing music that could've been played on a very,
very old record player. On a gramophone, even."

— JOY WILLIAMS, THE CIVIL WARS

"River"—Joni Mitchell

"Her vocals on this are particularly melancholy... It's
kind of taking the party down to a more pensive place.
This would be, like, around the time that you'd be having
a really heartfelt conversation with a family member or a
friend."

— ZOOEY DESCHANEL, SHE AND HIM

"Happiness Togetherness"—disco soul ballad by Heatwave

"This is the part of the evening that we might make a fire
in the fireplace, and then invite anyone who's too drunk
to drive to crash on the couch."

— CAROLINE POLACHEK, CHAIRLIFT

THE UNIVERSAL PLAYLIST

Note that in a pinch, the following types of music will work in all situations, during *any* phase of a dinner party:

a) INSTRUMENTALS. Jazz, classical, surf rock, Caribbean steel
drums, hip-hop remixes, Herb Alpert's faux-Mexican lounge

pop, minimalist hotel lobby electronica. They're all fine because there are no words to clash with—or distract from—your conversation. Exception: Bagpipe music. Do not play ever.

b) MUSIC IN A LANGUAGE YOU DON'T UNDERSTAND. Portuguese bossa nova tunes, Korean pop, Gaelic sea shanties. Even—if you don't speak English—Taylor Swift. This is one part of the party where not understanding what someone's saying is a *good* thing. Foreign language songs provide the comfort of a human voice, sans the distraction of comprehensible lyrics. They also subconsciously transport guests back to infancy, when words were just a soothing hum in the background as they awaited the original dinner party: mother's breast.

c) TONY BENNETT. There exist Michael Jackson haters. Even Sinatra tunes can divide a room. But *no one* hates Tony Bennett. We do not know why. Indeed, we urge Tony Bennett to leave his body to science so that we might one day discern the secret and use it to end war.

PART 3:
PREPARING THE APPETIZERS

You may feel that appetizer wisdom belongs in the chapter about food. But in fact *the second thing* a guest should encounter upon walking through your door[10] is something to nosh on. So by definition, you better have it ready *before* they walk through your door.

Appetizers are the preventative care of a dinner party. A sensible guest will not have eaten for hours. They will arrive not only hungry but with

---

10   The first: a cocktail (see next chapter).

their stomachs unlined—and therefore unfortified against the onslaught of booze to come. Left unfed, this person could have one martini and promptly become drunk, nauseous, and prone to looking up exes on Facebook. Get an appetizer in them, quickly.

The good news? Appetizers do not have to be fancy or expensive. Yes, you can get pricey olives in varying degrees of size, color, and salinity from an upscale Italian specialty store. But you can also get a couple of jars of those Spanish deals they sell cheap at Trader Joe's. Olives are mainly delivery vessels for salt. As long as the olives are salty, only the snobbiest guest will express dissatisfaction.

Ditto cheese. A special ornate cheese board laden with ten types of rare hunks from all corners of the world? That is certainly impressive and will be appreciated. But equally appreciated is a dinner plate with a block of cheddar from the supermarket down the street. Cheese is a fat delivery system. People like fats. Just get some out there. And crackers, guys. There are never enough crackers.

✦　✦　✦

> TEGAN: You're the person whose house I don't go to for dinner parties because I'm like, "They're just not good at it. I'm too hungry. I always have to go to McDonald's on the way home!"
> SARA: Oh my God, what a diva! Don't worry, I'll have lots of almonds for you, Tegan.
> — TEGAN AND SARA

✦　✦　✦

And that's pretty much all you need, appetizer-wise: something salty and something fatty.[11] Fatty cheese and salty olives. Fatty hummus and

---

11 Optional: Celery and carrot sticks to clean off your tongue between bites of various garlicky things. Note that at the end of the evening there will always be a handful of graying baby carrots left on the plate.

salty pita chips. Fatty seven-layer bean dip and the salty tears of self-loathing that come after downing a quart of it. Remove the items from any packaging, steer your guests to them, and you're done.

Of course, if you want to expend time and/or money on more elaborate starters, you're welcome to do so. Here are two of our personal standby recipes. Both are cheap, both are pretty easy, both have been deemed excellent by our friends or after years of peer-reviewed laboratory testing — whichever seems more plausible to you.

Brendan's Stuffed Fried Olives

One of a long line of European peasant dishes which Americans mistakenly think is fancy, this recipe comes courtesy of my longtime friend and cooking sensei Jolynn Deloach. As soon as Jolynn's party guests arrive, she puts them to work making these.[12] This isn't as hard to prepare as it sounds, and the work is offset by the fact that it is undoubtedly THE GREATEST THING YOU WILL EVER EAT IN YOUR LIFE.

Ingredients for filling:
    4 ounces ground pork
    4 ounces ground veal
    4 ounces chicken, shredded or minced
    1 quart tomato sauce (homemade, or use your favorite
       store-bought brand)
    Zest of 1 lemon
    1 teaspoon freshly grated nutmeg
    ½ cup grated Pecorino Romano

12 This is actually a classic host move; see chapter four, part one: "Conscript into Service."

6 slices good country bread, trimmed of crust and cut
   into ½ inch dice
2 eggs, beaten
1 box of tissues, because when people eat these jauns
   they are going to weep with joy

To assemble and fry:
40 large green olives (about 1½ cups; pitted are easier,
   but unpitted result in tastier orbs)
Flour, beaten egg, and dry bread crumbs for dredging
Vegetable oil (preferably peanut) for frying

Combine the meat with the tomato sauce and gently simmer
   until tender, around fifteen minutes. Be careful not to
   overcook it. When cool, shred or chop the meat finely. If
   you use a food processor, take care not to overmix — you
   want some texture.

Mix the rest of the filling ingredients together with the
   shredded meat. Form walnut-size balls of filling.

With a sharp knife, remove the flesh from the olive pits in one
   long spiral. (This is a lot easier with pre-pitted olives!)

Wrap the "corkscrew" of olive flesh around a ball of filling.
   Don't worry if it breaks; just patch it together around the
   filling.

Dredge each filled olive in flour, egg, and bread crumbs in
   preparation for frying.

Deep-fry at 350 degrees until golden brown and drain on
   brown paper or paper towels.

If the sheer boxer brief–dropping calorie count of these
   golden orbs has you worried your guests might quickly

become as stuffed as the olives themselves, simply limit the number you make. But honestly, you're all adults: it's okay if people spoil their dinner. Besides, you can always eat them like savory bonbons the next day, while you stream old episodes of *30 Rock* and make an appointment with your cardiologist.

Rico's Peperonata

This Italian specialty is something between a sauce and a stew, which you spoon onto hunks of crusty bread and eat the hell out of. Basically, what you're doing is turning healthy vegetables into sweet-and-sour olive-oily candy. By the way, I got this recipe from my actual Italian friend Francesco Malcangi, while I was visiting him in actual Italy, so you can tell everyone it's "authentic."

Ingredients:

> 4 bell peppers, each a different color: green, red, orange, yellow[13]
>
> 1 medium onion
>
> 2 stalks celery
>
> 2 medium tomatoes
>
> 1 cup good extra-virgin olive oil
>
> Bunch of salt
>
> 2 tablespoons granulated sugar
>
> 2 tablespoons balsamic vinegar

---

13 This is a purely show-off aesthetic move. Green peppers are fine if that's what you've got.

Slice the peppers into thin strips. Chop the onion coarsely.
Slice the celery widthwise into thin crescents. Chop up the
tomato coarsely. All this slicing and chopping is a pain in
the ass, but once it's done the rest goes quickly.

Add the olive oil to a deep saucepan over medium heat. Throw
in the celery and peppers, sprinkle liberally with salt, and
stir thoroughly till the veggies are coated. Cook them down
a bit, stirring occasionally, until they are slightly softened.
Then throw in the onion and tomatoes and a little more salt.
Cook for ten to fifteen minutes more, stirring occasionally.
Now you want the peppers to be getting *very* soft and
floppy.

Remove from the heat and stir in the sugar and vinegar. Taste.
Add more salt, vinegar, and sugar as needed.

Put back on the heat and turn it up high — you're now boiling
off any remaining water left in the veggies and making sure
they're all soft; you don't want anything crunchy in there.

Refrigerate overnight (or as long as you can before the party)
to get the flavors to meld as much as possible. Serve with
crusty bread. Also goes great mixed into scrambled eggs
the next morning. You're welcome.

CHAPTER FOUR

ARRIVALS

The doorbell rings. People have actually shown up. There is no escape. *Showtime.*

Hosts, at this point in the evening, keep one maxim in mind: *You should enjoy your own dinner party.*

Yes, you've poured energy and somewhere between a little and a ton of money into this. Yes, a bunch of people are going to use your toilet and judge your possessions. But be joyful! You picked your guests because you're interested in them, and now you get them all to yourself for several hours. Plus, you will eat, and everyone is going to compliment you on your cooking, including the stuff you accidentally burned (see chapter five). Also, if you're single, you may come out of this with a spouse.

As with flying, though, the most challenging part of a dinner party occurs at takeoff. Everyone is at their most sober and guarded. They may not feel safe enough to unbuckle their seat belts and walk freely about the cabin, so to speak. Your job at this moment is not to gorge on pâté and toast points, gurgle Châteauneuf-du-Pape, and loudly sing "New York State of Mind." You need to remain a functioning adult and guide the party to a cruising altitude where your *guests* are doing all that stuff. *Then* you can switch to autopilot and join in.

And with that, we have exhausted every air travel metaphor in our vocabulary and come to the point of this chapter: to help *you* help your *guests* quickly relax and chill while your party gets under way.

* ↟ *

"People are arriving and stomping off their boots at the bottom of the stairs. Lots of thick wool sweaters. It's mellow. I have a low-lighting kind of rule in my house. Someone is pouring wine. It's like an industrious focus on taking our sweet time."

— FEIST

* ↟ *

PART 1: FIRST THROUGH THE DOOR

As noted in chapter one, a gathering doesn't become a dinner party until at least four people are present.

So how do you deal with that awkward twilight zone you enter when the first guest arrives, and it's just the two of you standing there surrounded by crudités?

It's not a dinner party yet, with the happy buzz of group conversation. But neither is this a perfect time for easygoing, one-on-one shootin' the breeze. After all, a bunch more people are about to show up, and you likely have last-minute stuff to deal with: a ziti in the oven you must keep an eye on, a turntable that skips if you breathe near it. This is a time when a host is *preoccupied*.[1]

The trick to getting through this strange ten to fifteen minutes is to let the first guest feel acknowledged *even as you continue to prepare for and/or obsess about the party*. Some techniques:

---

1 Of course, if you've got literally everything ready for your party, exactly on time, you are totally free to treat this as easygoing shootin'-the-breeze time. But we must say we've never met any host who was totally ready exactly on time, so you may be a robot.

1. Make Them a Cocktail

This is the first thing to bestow upon *any* guest when they arrive (see this chapter, part two). But it is especially crucial that you do so for guest number one, as it accomplishes three goals simultaneously:

- Shows that you value and are paying attention to them, while also
- Allowing you to use them as a willing guinea pig on which to test-run your cocktail recipe,[2] plus
- Gets them tipsy, thus rendering the ensuing techniques way more likely to succeed.

2. Tell Them a Joke

We start each episode of *The Dinner Party Download* with a celebrity telling a quick, punny joke — an "icebreaker." We recommend you start *your* party by setting your guest at ease with icebreakers, too. Not because they're funny. But because they're terrible.

This was not what we expected, by the way. When we first came up with the icebreaker concept, we were hoping to revive what we saw as the dying art of joke telling. We quickly learned there is no such art; most jokes are awful.[3] But then we realized this makes them glorious.

No one *expects* jokes to be good. In fact, a successful joke *is one that fails.* The desired response is not a laugh but a groan. It is the form of comedy for which the bar is set lowest... and is therefore the easiest for everyone to participate in. Your three-year-old tells jokes. Your ninety-year-old grandmother tells jokes. The douchebag who drunkenly hits on you at the bar tells jokes. If we could translate barks, we bet we'd discover that dogs are

---

2   Let them *know* it's a test run. Make them feel they're involved in the process. Use words like "let's" and "we" — "Should we give this cocktail recipe a dry run?" Best part: If they're aware that you're still in experimenting mode, the drink doesn't even have to be good.

3   Professional stand-up comedians disdainfully call them "street jokes." That's how low an opinion they have of them — like, gutter-level low.

mostly telling jokes.[4] Jokes are the great populist equalizer of comedy. Just about every guest at your party can safely and easily join in.

Furthermore, when you, the host, start the evening with a mega-lame joke, it sends a bunch of excellent messages to the guest: that humor will be appreciated tonight. That no one should take themselves too seriously. And that total failure will be celebrated.[5]

Here's an easy and very extremely bad icebreaker to get you started.

> Q: What do you do when you see a space man?
> A: You park it in it, man.
> — HUGH BONNEVILLE, DOWNTON ABBEY'S
> LORD GRANTHAM

3. Induce a Monologue

We'll talk later about having great conversations with your guests. But here at the beginning of your party, you've got too much on your mind for that. What you want to do is inspire your guest to *monologue*. At length. Freeing you to cook or clean while they sit nearby and ramble. This can actually be pleasant—chopping onions feels way less onerous if you do it while someone's filling you in on juicy work gossip.

Speaking of which, yes, if your guest is a coworker, asking about juicy work gossip is a fine way to provoke a monologue. A few other phrases that do the trick:

> "So, tell me all about your vacation in [insert name of foreign locale here]."

---

4   Three barks is the joke. The bark after that is them going "BADUMP-BUMP."
5   Another smooth move: Tailor the joke to the guest. Precede this by saying, "Hey, I think *you'll* appreciate this one." When Brendan was a teen he had an uncle who'd always pull him aside at parties and do this. The ensuing joke was often vaguely dirty. It made Brendan feel like a grown-up.

"Is little [name of guest's child] still [insert disturbing behavior here] at school?"

"How's the divorce coming along?"[6]

If the guest is a Single and Proud, you're in luck. Just ask them about their date last night and you'll unleash an hour of nonstop entertainment. As for Narcissists and Comedians, you don't even have to prompt them; they'll be monologuing the second they enter your home.

4. Conscript into Service

But perhaps your first guest is not a drinker, doesn't really "get" jokes, and isn't much of a talker to boot. Perhaps this early arriver is the guy from your office you invited on a lark, and it turns out he's a taciturn Seventh-day Adventist[7] (see sidebar "A Note on Nondrinkers").

That's fine. To make sure he doesn't feel ignored while you flit about, get him *involved*. Have him *help* with the prep work. It's a double win: He feels included, and both of you, absorbed in your respective tasks, have an excuse not to actually interact much.[8]

Plus, bonus: You get a free handyman for fifteen minutes! This is because most people who show up first to dinner parties tend to be Eager Beavers at heart—the kind of folks who *live* to help hosts. Go ahead and

---

6   One more tempting phrase: "Did you hear about [insert Trump's latest executive order here]?" AVOID. The resulting monologue will dominate all conversation for the rest of the party. We'll get to the political talk later.

7   BTW, here's an alcohol-free "mocktail" invented for our show by Pamela Vaughn at Clara's on the River in Battle Creek, Michigan, and *inspired* by the teetotaling Seventh-day Adventist John Harvey Kellogg—the coinventor of cornflakes. In a blender, place 1 cup milk, 5 dried dates, 3 tablespoons cornflakes, 1 tablespoon honey, 1 scoop ice. Blend. Garnish with more flakes. We admit that it sounds brunchy, but we figure that's trumped by the conversational value of handing a Seventh-day Adventist the only Seventh-day-Adventist-themed drink ever.

8   Remember Brendan's cooking sensei Jolynn? She had this move *down*.

tell them to set the table. Or shuck corn. Or rewire the dining room light fixture. They'll find all this delightful. Chances are they even keep a refrigerator-size tool kit in their SUV, because "you never know when you'll need a wire stripper."

Occasionally, though, the early arriver is just a Hipster who's got somewhere cooler to be later. They've arrived early because they plan to bail early. You can lure these types into helping by stroking their aesthete's ego: just treat them like impromptu design consultants. "You've got such a good eye; show me how *you'd* slice and arrange all this cheese." "What do you think: would the couch look better by the window? It would? I think you're *totally right.* Here, let's move it."

> Q: What do you get when you drop a piano into a mine shaft?
> A: A-flat miner.
> — RIVERS CUOMO, WEEZER

5. The Doorman Endgame

A knock at the door — more guests have arrived! You're almost through the twilight zone! Now for your final move: telling the first guest to do you a favor and greet the new arrivals.

This serves two functions. You get a few precious seconds alone to make sure everything looks ready, to adjust your makeup, or to discreetly pop a Xanax. And meanwhile, your guests are forced to hang out and bond for a moment without you, getting them used to the idea that you won't be able to attend to them every freaking second of the evening.

At this point, bring this phase of your party to a close by sweeping in to further facilitate the bonding process. Tell each guest something complimentary and conversation-worthy about the other. Perhaps toss in another joke. And *definitely* hand these sober new arrivals some cocktails. Hey! Since we're on the subject:

PART 2: COCKTAILS

Oh, alcohol. Untier of tongues, breaker of ice, loosener of neckwear and libidos. You are the speedway to conversation and merriment, and a host's best friend. Of course, you are also, potentially, a host's worst enemy (see chapter three, "The Bad Drunk"), but we'll worry about that later. For now, the important thing is to get a cocktail in your guest's hand, quickly.

Why specifically start with cocktails, you ask? Why not beer or wine? What a great question, to which we happen to have a ton of answers.

1. Pacing

At a party, you want your guests to *hit the ground drinking*. That is to say, the strongest booze — liquor — should be deployed first. This is a) so that everyone loosens up with maximum speed, and b) so that, when they leave the party several hours later, they have sobered up enough to pilot a vehicle/not fall off a subway platform.

2. Delineation

There is the plain old daytime world. Then there is the fantastic Technicolor playtime of the dinner party. And in modern Western society, there is no more iconic dividing line between the two than the first sip of a cocktail.

For Generation Xers, this can be a hard concept to grasp. You were brought up bombarded with TV commercials portraying *beer* as the symbolic beverage of evening and post-work celebration. "Tonight," the commercials said, "let it be Löwenbräu." After a hard day on the job, they said, "It's Miller time."

These are *falsehoods* and *propaganda*. There are *many* times which can be Miller time. You can totally drink beer in the middle of the day at a baseball park. You can have a beer with nachos at Chili's, in the midst of Saturday afternoon underwear shopping at the mall. You might even get away with a glass of beer on your lunch break at work.

But unless you are somehow reading this book in the boozy *Mad Men* days of 1963,[9] you do not sip cocktails until the workday is over. Similarly, you don't typically mix Manhattans at an afternoon picnic. And during Sunday morning football watching at the sports bar, you don't order martinis with your buffalo chicken dip.

What we're saying is, it is liquor which belongs *specifically* to the evening. So when a host puts a cocktail in a guest's hand, it's the universal

9   And if you are, buy and store as many examples of midcentury furniture as you can; in a few decades it'll be worth a fortune.

indicator that day is officially done[10] — and as they say in New Orleans,[11] *laissez les bon temps rouler.*

3. Practicality

A half hour to an hour into your party, we promise, you get to stop being hosty, and are allowed to become guesty. Your attendees having been loosened up, your pork loin now out of the oven and resting safely on the stove top, you can pour *yourself* a drink. And perhaps another. Etcetera.

Of course, professional cocktailians[12] are *used* to whipping up drinks for others whilst becoming intoxicated themselves. But *you* are *not* a professional cocktailian. If you were, you wouldn't be reading this book, because cocktailians don't throw dinner parties; their workdays *begin* at 5 p.m., and the rest of the time they either sleep or get tattoos.

As an amateur, then, you want to do any cocktail mixing early in the evening, while you're still sober enough to reliably add up measurements in your head, and can also remember to put the lid back on a shaker full of booze *before* shaking it up. Save the preparation-free beer and wine for later, when you're Drunky Brewster.

4. Liquor Before Beer, Never Fear

Come on, guys. You know this.

---

10 Exception: When it happens at brunch. Fuck that noise.

11 Note: New Orleans exists in a state of perpetual 24-7 dinner party. Therefore, you will encounter cocktails there at *all* hours. We mean that literally: in New Orleans there is never an hour during which you will not be encountering cocktails.

12 We prefer this term to the popular "mixologist." "Mixologist" seems a more appropriate descriptor of an organic chemist, or a dub reggae DJ. Whereas "cocktailian" not only has the word "cocktail" right in it, it also kind of has the word "alien." Which, if you've ever seen a cocktailian in full steampunk gear, trying and failing to hold a conversation with a normal earthling during daylight hours, is entirely apt.

Each episode of *The Dinner Party Download* features a different cocktailian showing off a different custom cocktail recipe. Often these concoctions feature exotic elixirs from foreign lands, with fabulous names we can barely pronounce. *Falernum. Dimmi Milano. Ochos Sientos Sotol. Peenie Wallie.*[13]

Or sometimes we get a cocktailian calling for the use of special nonalcoholic ingredients which no one with a day job has time to track down or create. Homemade vanilla-coconut simple syrup. Canned jackfruit. Or how about Aleppo pepper extract, which you'll need to order from an online chemical supplier?

And then there are the recipes that specify the use of ultrarare liquors, available almost nowhere. The most egregious example being the British bartender who found a bottle of unlabeled, unidentifiable mystery spirit gathering dust in the back of his bar, and used it as the base of his cocktail for us. Thanks for that, dude.

To judge from our show, then, the making of cocktails requires one thousand bottles

> *So two cupcakes are sitting in an oven. And one cupcake says to the other cupcake, "Man, it's hot in here." And the other cupcake goes, "OH MY GOD, A TALKING CUPCAKE!!"*
> — JONAH HILL

of weird and/or pricey liquors, a pantry full of exotic fruits and herbs, and a home laboratory. The good news: NOT TRUE.

Yes, as show hosts, we like it when bartenders whip up astoundingly complex creations, because it's fun to watch artists work at a high level. But here's our dirty little secret: After work, we order dry martinis. Which is more or

---

13   Yes, there is (or at least was—it's impossible to find on sale online anymore) a real thing called *Peenie Wallie*. It's Jamaican peanut cream liqueur. Blend with wine[13a] and you have a liquid PBJ.

13a   Do not actually do this.

less cold gin in a glass. As far as *we're* concerned, if you've got the building blocks for a martini on hand, your home liquor cabinet is complete.

Of course, your guests may have slightly broader tastes. So here's a list of a mere nine bottles of alcohol—plus some cheap mixers, garnishes, and equipment—from which you can concoct a surprising variety of classic tipples.

ALCOHOLS:

London Dry Gin

For use in martinis, the most bestest of all cocktails (see sidebar "The Perfect Martini").

Many people will tell you they prefer vodka to gin. They don't understand that gin is basically vodka infused with actual flavor. Anyway, don't worry about those people. Have gin on hand for when *we* come over.

Dry Vermouth

The only other alcohol that can conceivably be added to a true martini. Whether it *should* be is, of course, a point of fierce contention among martini drinkers. (Winston Churchill's recipe called for gin, followed by only a "bow in the direction of France.") Which is actually a great reason to have vermouth around: to kick off some good-natured sparring among your guests, over a subject of zero actual consequence.

*   ✦ *

"I do think the reason why people started dumping the vermouth is because it's the least alcoholic part of [a martini], right? It has the lowest ABV, or proof, to it. When you're talking about Churchill or Hemingway... they were great men in many ways, but they are not examples of the best types of drinkers. They drank way too much, and they'd prefer the alcohol. Now, I like to

drink, too, so I don't want to totally knock them down.
But to me, the vermouth is a civilizing agent."
— WASHINGTON, DC'S "BARTENDER IN CHIEF," DEREK BROWN,
MAKER OF WHAT GQ ONCE NAMED "THE BEST MARTINI IN AMERICA"

Vodka

Vodka's super popular. So you need to have some around, even though we have issues with it because everyone thinks it can be substituted for gin in martinis. FACT: When vodka is substituted for gin in a martini, *it is no longer a martini*. Someone should come up with a name for whatever it is. An "Abomination"? Something.

Admittedly, vodka—which in its rye or wheat-based varieties is ideally flavorless—is great for mixing with just about anything. Also, you'll need it to make vodka and sodas, the diet drink of the cocktail world. If you've invited an actor or fashion model to your party, don't even bother asking if they want a vodka and soda. They want one. Have it ready.

> ❦ **VODKA SODA**[14] ❦
>
> Over ice, pour
> 1½ to 2 ounces vodka
> 4 to 5 ounces soda

Bourbon

In an ideal world, every American would have universal health care and a bottle each of bourbon, Scotch, and rye whiskey. But if you can only afford

---

14 Except where noted, classic cocktail recipes kindly provided by award-winning cock-tailian superhero Cari Hah, of Alcove Big Bar in Los Angeles.

BRENDAN FRANCIS NEWNAM

RICO GAGLIANO

one,[15] split the difference by going for a "high rye content" bourbon like Bulleit or Michter's. Spicier than standard bourbon, it'll still work as the classic base of a Manhattan. But it also makes a decent substitute for rye or cognac in a Sazerac[16]—arguably the oldest American cocktail. Speaking of which, the Sazerac's "authenticity" makes it the perfect drink to serve to the Hipster at your party. Just understand in advance that no matter how successfully you pull it off, the Hipster will have had a better one a couple of weeks ago in New Orleans.

❦ SAZERAC ❦

3 to 4 dashes Peychaud's bitters
White sugar cube
Capful soda water
2 ounces high rye bourbon
Few drops absinthe
Lemon peel

Put bitters in a mixing glass.
Add sugar cube and soda water and crush into a sludge.
Add bourbon.
Add ice. Stir.
Coat a second glass with the absinthe.
Strain the bourbon mixture into it.
Squeeze lemon peel over the top and serve.

15   One type of *whiskey*, we mean. If the choice is between whiskey and health care, go for the health care.

16   Note: A Sazerac also calls for a tiny bit of absinthe. Long unavailable in the U.S., absinthe became briefly hip when it reappeared a few years ago, until people realized you have to shell out over a hundred bucks to get one that tastes good. A midpriced bottle is all you need for Sazeracs, though. It should last you the rest of your life, unless you are a painter in France.

Sweet Vermouth

For Manhattans.

2 ounces high rye bourbon
1 ounce sweet vermouth
2 to 3 dashes Angostura bitters
Luxardo cherry

Put everything in a mixing glass.
Add ice and stir until chilled.
Strain into a chilled cocktail glass.
Drop in a cherry.

Campari

For making the classic Negroni, in which three strong flavors (bitter Campari, herby gin, and sweet vermouth) combine to create something magically balanced. Maybe this is why bartenders like mixing Negronis: it makes them feel like Dumbledore or something.

❧ NEGRONI ❧

1 ounce Campari
1 ounce sweet vermouth (½ ounce if you're using Carpano Antica)
1 ounce gin

Add to a glass and drop in a large ice cube.

Tequila Blanco

For use in margaritas—officially the most popular cocktail in America.[17] Hey, it's a tasty melted lime Popsicle that gets you drunk; we understand. Normally, margaritas also require triple sec, but you can do without it if you splurge a little on *really good* tequila. So in this case, splurge a little.

❧ TOMMY'S MARGARITA ❧

As invented by Julio Bermejo of Tommy's Mexican Restaurant in San Francisco.

2 ounces 100 percent agave blanco tequila

1 ounce *fresh* lime juice

½ ounce agave nectar

Shake over ice.

Pour into a glass (with or without salted rim).

Fill the glass with more ice and serve.

Sparkling Wine

A.k.a. champagne or prosecco. Often used to top off cocktails, including the classic French 75. Bonus: You can serve it neat to guests who hate liquor.

---

17   Source: The 2017 On-Premise Consumer Survey by Nielsen CGA. Yes, Nielsen collects data on what TV we watch *and* what cocktails we order. They know *all about* our preferred means of sloth.

FRENCH 75

1 ounce gin
½ ounce lemon juice
½ ounce simple syrup
Sparkling wine
Lemon twist

Shake gin, lemon juice, and syrup over ice.
Strain into a champagne flute.
Top with sparkling wine.
Add a lemon twist.

One Bottle of Something No One's Ever Heard Of

Next time you find yourself overseas,[18] instead of a souvenir snow globe,
bring home a bottle of the
locals' favorite booze. The
weirder the better. A spirit dis-
tilled from poison ivy? Excellent! Rice liquor infused with
fermented snake venom? Perf!
Don't worry, you don't have to
taste it, or even open it. Just display it and get some conversation going.
Bonus points if the label is handwritten in a foreign language and/or the
bottle is shaped like a monkey.

> Q: Why couldn't the lifeguard save
> the hippie?
> A: 'Cause he was too far out, man.
> — CHRISTOPHER OWENS, INDIE
> ROCKER

---

18   Don't get overseas much? Not to worry, there's plenty of weird booze to be found right
here in America. Example: Malört. Beloved in Chicago, this is a bitter, Swedish-style
wormwood liqueur that even the label once admitted is "unrelenting (even brutal) to the
palate."

MIXERS:

Ice

If you make a lot of cocktails, you'll go through ice like America goes through fossil fuels. So when you wake up the morning of your party, your first order of business is to fill all the ice cube trays you have with water and get them in the freezer. Then buy a bag of ice for backup. If you don't have enough room for it in the freezer, that's a great excuse to clean out your freezer. You need ice more than you need that jelly jar filled with rendered bacon fat from two years ago.

Peychaud's and Angostura Bitters

Many cocktail recipes call for a few dashes of one of these bitters, even though no one really knows exactly what's in them. For real—literally five people on Earth know the secret proprietary formula for Angostura.[19] Supposedly one base ingredient is nutmeg, though, which in large doses can be a laxative and a hallucinogen...and that's just the ingredient we've heard about. *Do not drink in large doses.*

Tonic

Mix with gin, add a slice of lime, and wham, you're a fancy Englishman. Yes, yes, it also works with vodka, if you must. You are welcome to buy upscale specialty tonic handcrafted by local artisans for fifteen dollars an ounce. But a plastic two-liter of Schweppes also works—just go easy on it 'cause it's loaded with sugar.

---

19   Rumor has it these five people never travel on planes together, lest a crash cause the recipe to be lost to the ages. Seriously.

Lemon and Lime Juice

Squeezing fresh lemons or limes is the way to go but can be labor-intensive if you're making a lot of cocktails, so bottled *pure* lemon or lime juice can be okay in a pinch. Avoid those little plastic fruit-shaped squeezy things: the juice inside comes from concentrate and is adulterated with stuff that changes the flavor. If you accidentally bought little plastic fruit-shaped squeezy things, empty and wash them out and give them to kids for use as squirt guns.

Simple Syrup

This involves cooking and is thus an oxymoron—it seems to us that *actually* simple syrup comes in a squat bottle and has the word "MAPLE" on the side.[20]

Still, "simple" syrup is a common way to add sugar to a drink, without sugar crystals forming a grainy, wet rock candy at the bottom of your glass. The standard recipe is indeed pretty easy: Heat one part water in a sauce-pan, add one part sugar, stir until dissolved, and store in the fridge. It'll keep for a month.

Agave Nectar

For margaritas.

Club Soda

For vodka sodas. Or add a dash of bitters and lemon to create a vaguely cocktaily beverage for the nondrinkers (see sidebar "A Note on Nondrinkers").

---

20 Of course, you *can* buy simple syrup for, like, twelve dollars a bottle at Sur La Table. That makes the name more appropriate, but may also mean you're way too rich. Consider making homemade syrup and donating that money to charity instead.

GARNISHES:

Olives

The third and final classic ingredient in a martini. We favor standard, briny, unadorned green cocktail olives. But olives stuffed with pimento, blue cheese, garlic, cashews, jalapeño, methamphetamine, or whatever the kids are putting in them these days can serve as alluring "training wheels" for the martini novice.

Luxardo Cherries

Not to be confused with those radioactive-orange maraschino cherries beloved by five-year-olds, these are syrupy, dark red, sweet-and-sour little stemless orbs. They are the magnificent reward for getting to the bottom of any drink into which they have been dropped (e.g., a Manhattan). Scientific truth: Convince a guest to eat a Luxardo cherry atop a piece of salty cheese on a cracker, and they will be 75 percent more likely to sleep with you.

Lemon, Orange, and Lime Wedges/Twists

You'll need the limes for gin and tonics. A lemon twist will top off your French 75, and will brighten up that super boring vodka and soda.

We also grudgingly acknowledge that FDR liked a lemon twist along with an olive in his martini, and Queen Elizabeth II reportedly likes three slices of lemon in hers. So putting lemon in martinis is an okay thing to do, as long as you're a powerful world leader of immense historic importance.

EQUIPMENT:

Shaker and Jigger

Head to any modern American city center. Look for the vinyl record store— the one right next to the vintage clothing outlet. Take a left, and then shield your eyes from the bright gleam of hammered brass ice buckets through a store-front window. You've found it! One of America's new-look bartending stores. In addition to top-shelf boozes from around the globe, these joints feature shelves and shelves of tantalizing glass and metal barware. Special stirrers. Squeezers. Vintage glass cocktail shakers. Beautifully machine-tooled silver toothpicks for olive spearing. Tiny blowtorches for setting drinks aflame.

Admire these objects. Stroke them fetishistically and dream of being able to afford them. Then leave, go to Target, and spend twenty bucks on a stainless steel seventeen-ounce cocktail shaker and a jigger that measures one, one and a half, and half-ounce increments. They're fine for most needs.

Glassware

Cocktail recipes usually call for the drink to be served in a specific kind of glass—highball, lowball, coupe, champagne flute, etcetera. There are very good reasons for this, but unless you're about to be married and can therefore get others to gift you ten different sets of glassware, we say it's fine to make do with whatever glasses you have. Or even buy disposable cups if you're a super broke college grad. Just be aware that no matter how small your party is, or how many little plastic martini glasses you buy, over the course of the evening your guests will end up using *all* of them. And then they'll use all the glasses in your cupboards. By the end of the night you will be drinking booze out of coffee mugs, finger bowls, empty Activia yogurt containers...really, any vessel that can hold liquid. We don't know why this is, but it's best to just accept it.

Coasters

By all means, protect your wooden surfaces by setting out cocktail coasters if you want. Just please avoid cardboard coasters swiped from the bar down the street, which advertise Camel cigarettes and/or the new album from Keith Urban. Coasters advertising our show are fine, though.

* ⋏ *

*"I would first urge you to never turn to violence as a first
resort to any question. I always say 'Hug before punch.'
Perhaps gather your guest in a bearlike embrace, and
gently explain to them that this wood would appreciate
their love as much as it is loving us."*

— ACTOR (AND WOODWORKER) NICK OFFERMAN, ON WHETHER

TO PUNCH SOMEONE WHO SETS A DRINK, SANS COASTER,

ON A NICE PIECE OF FURNITURE

* ⋏ *

THE WISDOM OF BATCHING

There are many upsides to serving cocktails. Ease of preparation is not always among them. There are liquids to be measured. Lemons to be cut or squeezed. And it's surprising how painfully cold a steel shaker full of ice and booze can become. Like, stethoscope-on-your-nipples cold.

Speaking of shakers: even big ones will only hold enough booze to mix *maybe* four drinks at a time. To serve a party of twelve guests a couple of cocktails each, you'll have to repeat the mixing process *six times in a row*. This you must do while keeping the small talk going, providing directions to your tardy guests via speakerphone, and making sure dinner doesn't explode.

> Q: What's the difference between an old Greyhound bus station and a lobster with a boob job?
> A: One's a crusty bus station, and the other's a busty crustacean.
>
> — MACKENZIE DAVIS, ACTOR

That may be your jam. If not, the typical solution is to designate a pal, significant other, or guest to help make the drinks.

But there's another solution: Before the party, just *pre*mix a big jug of your favorite cocktail. Then just chill or dilute the booze with ice as needed when you serve each glassful. Yay: now you can *talk* to your guests, instead of shouting at them over the sound of your endless cocktail shaking.

YOUR OTHER OPTION: PUNCH

Yes, we know. For many, punch brings to mind parties of the dusty past: people in blazers and dresses standing around a big bowl of fruity, neon-red liquid, sipping it from little glass teacups until someone dons a lampshade.

Okay—and your problem with that is what, exactly?

A bowlful of punch is pretty much the classic symbol of a dinner party, and combines the high octane of liquor with the practicality of self-service. Whip up a couple of gallons in advance, set it out with cups and a ladle, and you're done.

Just remember: Since punch tends to be fruity and goes down smoother than most cocktails, your guests will drink more of it, faster. And since they're serving themselves, you (and likely they) will quickly lose track of how much they've had. To avoid everyone getting Keith Richards–level hammered before you've even served the meal, keep the alcohol content a little lower.

Here's a recipe for a colonial-era punch that will make you proud to be an American, and will also make you the right amount drunk. It comes to us courtesy of Jim Hewes, bartender at the famed Round Robin Bar at the Willard, the historic Washington, DC, hotel where the term "lobbyist" was supposedly coined. You can taste the corrupting influence of special interest groups in every drop.

❧ FISH HOUSE PUNCH ❧

2 parts rum
1 part brandy
1 part triple sec
2 parts lemon sour mix
Several dashes grenadine

Pour over ice and dilute with club soda and orange juice to taste. Yes, we're aware that only one ingredient in this thing is on our list of suggested items for your liquor cabinet, and that's club soda. But since you're serving everyone punch, you don't need that other stuff[21] *now*.

---

21 Even so, have gin, dry vermouth, and olives available in case we come over. It's the public radio equivalent of keeping an empty chair at the Passover table for Elijah.

❧ THE PERFECT MARTINI ❧

By this point in the chapter, you've probably realized that we're martini drinkers. But while the two of us are in complete agreement that the martini is, with the possible exception of naps, the greatest invention of all time, each of us insists upon *extremely specific* preparations for our respective martinis. Not unlike James Bond, if James Bond was a podcast nerd instead of a licensed assassin.

MARTINI "RICO"

3 ounces Plymouth gin

Barspoonful dry vermouth

Olives

Chill a small martini glass. Coat the inside with vermouth and discard the excess. Shake the gin over ice. Strain into a glass and garnish with a spear of three olives.

MARTINI "BRENDAN"

3 ounces Beefeater gin

Barspoonful dry vermouth

Olives

Chill a small martini glass. Coat the inside with vermouth and discard the excess. Stir the gin over ice. Strain into a glass and garnish with a spear of three olives.

*   *   *

You may notice the only difference between these recipes is the type of gin and whether it is shaken or stirred. Feel free to try both recipes before realizing that mine is the best. — Rico

No, mine is the best. — Brendan

Stop it with your unending lies. — Rico

Really? We're doing this here, in front of everybody? — Brendan

Okay. — Rico

But mine is the best. — Rico

STOP. Mine. — Brendan

WHEN TO START WINE-ING

Being a "good drinker" means knowing how to socially lubricate and feel euphoric without becoming a slurring zombie or dessert barfer who wakes up near dead. And the secret to being a good drinker is knowing how and when to downshift from cocktails[22] to wine[23].

Though it pains us to write this, we suggest making the pivot after one cocktail. Truth be told, *we* sometimes pivot after two, but this is a case where what's good for the goose will make the gander sleepy and belligerent.

Once you've downed your cocktail, have a glass of water. Much of the appeal of social drinking is simply having a prop to fill your hands and your time. Water allows you to pour, sip, or excuse-yourself-for-a-refill-when-someone-gets-inappropriate just as much as a second cocktail does. Once you've rehydrated, you're ready for wine.

WHICH WINES TO WINE

The rule of thumb about drinking wine is, *there is no longer a rule of thumb about drinking wine.* Guests can drink any color wine they want, with any type of food they want. Strive to have both colors on hand so they can pick.[24]

If you really want a wine that pairs exactly with your menu, ask the folks at your local wineshop. Unlike baristas and ex-boyfriends, they won't

---

22 Some A-level drinkers skip cocktails altogether and begin with champagne or sparkling wine. Sparklers are festive, lower alcohol, and the bubbles are a natural deterrent to overguzzling.

23 This might also be the time, if you're a beer drinker, to shift to beer. A crisp, blond pilsner is probably your most versatile choice, although there are a zillion beers out there now, and we're sure there's a book near where you bought this one, written by a dude with a full beard who can explain the differences.

24 To add an element of spectacle, and to make the proceedings that much more festive, consider a magnum or even a jeroboam of wine. These oversize bottles are sometimes a good value, always a good prop for Instagram, and you get to shout "JEROBOAM" all night.

judge you and are happy to help. But for those who don't care about how much rain fell in the Languedoc in 2013, there are some versatile crowd-pleasing wines that go with almost anything, all night long.

Reds

Try lighter grapes like Gamay, Dolcetto, or certain Pinot Noirs. Perf for surf *or* turf,[25] these are easily drinkable reds capable of pleasing both aficionados and people who don't know what the word "aficionado" means.

Whites

For whites, go with sauvignon blanc or French Chardonnay. They'll hold up to most foods except the beefiest beef. But be warned: If the weather is hot, they go down smoother than silk—and silk is *really* smooth, guys. Monitor your inebriation levels.

WHEN TO STOP WINE-ING

Spirits—the boozy kind—should probably not reappear until dessert is served, at which point a digestif of bourbon, cognac, or sherry can add a luscious edge to end-of-night proceedings. But it's not for everyone. Take a quick inventory: Are your guests speech-impaired? Is that your one friend's hand on your other friend's husband's knee? Are designated drivers unable to drive? If the answer to all these questions is "No," proceed.

---

25 Not 100 percent true but we just wanted to say that phrase in print.

Dessert is also the time to offer coffee, tea, or herbal tea to the drivers, or to any guests who are fans of their livers.

✦ ✦ ✦

"You're responsible for the clothing you wear, in any situation where people are going to be hugging while holding glasses of liquids...I mean, look, I don't go into any public environment unless I'm wearing a dark suit, in which case [spilled] wine doesn't matter."

— *Alton Brown, on appropriate drinking attire*

✦ ✦ ✦

A NOTE ON NONDRINKERS

Some of your guests may choose not to drink. They may or may not care to tell you why. Either way, as a host, your job is TO NOT MAKE A BIG DEAL OUT OF IT.

Treat the nondrinker the same way you would any other guest. Are you serving everyone a second round of cocktails? Serve the nondrinker a second glass of club soda and lemon. No further drama is necessary.

By the same token, don't worry about being tipsy — or fueling other guests' tipsiness — in the presence of a nondrinker. Generally speaking, nondrinkers know what they're in for at a dinner party, and you're not "leaving them out" of anything. Though they don't get to experience the entertainment of a righteous buzz, they do get the entertainment of watching the drinkers make mild jackasses of themselves. Plus, free food.

And if you yourself are a nondrinker, that's equally cool. Since a dinner party is a reflection of your personality and your beliefs, you are well within your rights to throw a boozeless party. Just let guests know in advance, so they don't bring wine (see sidebar "Dining Rules for Guests"). And also be aware that it will be approximately 50 percent more difficult to get people to chill. You will therefore want to memorize 50 percent more icebreakers and 50 percent more Small Talk anecdotes.

PART 3: SMALL TALK

Okay, the booze is flowing. Now to make the conversation follow suit. For this, you need to deploy some small talk.

Small Talk precedes more substantive conversations (see chapter six, "Conversation") which will happen later in the evening. Despite its diminutive name, Small Talk serves a huge purpose: It gives guests a chance to get to know one another and take one another's measure before the conversation turns to weightier matters—e.g., sex, the lonely meaninglessness of existence, and Trump's latest tweet. Small Talk whets the conversational appetite. It's like stretching before a jog, jogging before a run, or running before cardiac arrest.

With some luck, a few of your guests will turn out to be champion small talkers. If so, just put cocktails in their hands and let them have at it, while you go check on the roast. But if not, you'll need to get the small talk ball rolling yourself. Some dos and don'ts:

DOs

The goal of excellent Small Talk is to *not offend anyone* whilst simultaneously *blowing everyone's minds with stuff they don't already know about.*

Traditionally, of course, Small Talk has involved specifically *not* blowing people's minds. The evils of traffic and the weather—these are said to be the mainstays of small talk. For us, this is akin to showing up to a non-Scottish dinner party to find everyone wearing the same drab plaid. Or listening to an a cappella choir in which everyone is singing the same notes. It's *boring*. Inoffensive conversation need not also be soporific.

So we recommend scouring newspapers and the Internet for what we call "bright shiny conversational objects." News items and trivia that people likely *haven't* heard about. Stuff that'll immediately grab a guest's imagination and get the rhetorical juices[26] flowing. We start every show discussing such items, and four hundred episodes later, we have it down to a science. Here are three story types that make for fail-safe small talk.

Small Talk Type 1: Science Stories

Every day, all over the world, teams of people who did not spend their college years chugging Pabst are hypothesizing, testing their hypotheses, and publishing the results in obscure publications like the *Journal for Emu Testicular Fortitude*. Their intention is to expand the boundaries of human understanding and/or invent a drug that will earn shareholders billions of dollars. Either way, the by-product of their labor is that you get to make awesome small talk about it.

> *So a grasshopper walks into a bar. And the bartender goes, "Hey, y'know, we've got a drink named after you." And the grasshopper goes, "Really?! You've got a drink named Bob?!"*
>
> — HEATHER HAVRILESKY,
> AUTHOR AND ADVICE COLUMNIST

The wonderful thing about science stories is that, unlike politics, pop culture criticism, or the question "Why doesn't America have consistent cellular phone reception

---

26 Not to be confused with Rhetorical Juicy Juice™, which contains only 10 percent real rhetoric.

decades after the freaking technology was invented?" science often provides us with *actual answers*. Nice, objective facts and data are fine things to discuss during initial conversations with strangers. There will be plenty of time for wildly subjective opinions later.

P.S.: Science stories will even be enjoyed by the new breed of anti-science skeptics, as long as the research being discussed is mildly ridiculous and/or involves an undeniably cute animal. A couple of true stories, by way of example:

Music to Neuter Cats To

A 2015 article in the *Journal of Feline Medicine* described a study of a dozen pet cats that were being neutered. During surgery, the cats were fitted with headphones and exposed to various genres of music. These included two minutes each of Samuel Barber's Adagio for Strings (Opus 11), Natalie Imbruglia's "Torn," and AC/DC's "Thunderstruck."

The point of the study was to determine which type of music most relaxed the cats,[27] and would thus allow veterinarians to use lower, less dangerous doses of anesthetic during feline surgery. The point of bringing this up at a dinner party, of course, is to squee over the idea of cats wearing teeny headphones and listening to metal.

Why the Fuck?

Here's why the fuck: *Cursing dulls pain.*

According to research by Richard Stephens of Keele University in England, uttering cuss words activates the body's fight-or-flight response. This leads to a surge of adrenaline, which has a pain-numbing effect. Ste-

---

27 For the record, classical music relaxed cats the most, whereas AC/DC got them pumped up and ready to play defensive tackle in a kitty football game.

phens found, for example, that people who swear can hold their hands in ice water for twice as long as people who don't.

Lest you think this means that Richard Pryor could jump through a plate-glass window without feeling it, Stephens also found that cursing loses its magical numbing power if you do it all the time. Apparently, "chain-swearers" (science-ese for "potty mouths") become inured to the anesthetic benefits of swearing. So if you're a chain-swearer, the next time you hit your thumb with a hammer, shout something you *wouldn't* normally shout. Like "Crank up the Coldplay."

Small Talk Type 2: New Portmanteaus

Portmanteaus, of course, are hybrid terms like "jazzercise," "fanzine," and "Brangelina." Two words smashed together to describe an invention, event, or phenomenon for which there is, as yet, no other word. That's why new portmanteaus make great small talk fodder; by their nature, they get you talking about something so new that society hasn't even really figured out what to call it yet.

We love portmanteaus so much that we originally called our show *Brendco Gagliewnam*, until we received a cease-and-desist letter from a Hungarian cheese concern. A few of our favorite recent portmanteaus:

"Blow-Tox"

Some curly-haired people pay top dollar for blowouts — a beauty procedure whereby hair is artificially straightened. The problem: Sweating can cause the straightened hair to frizz right back up again. Enter "Blow-Tox," in which Botox is injected into the scalp, near the hairline, inhibiting sweating and thus preserving the blowout.

Advocates argue that the $650 procedure is cheaper than doling out $125 for a blowout every time you break a sweat. No word on whether we can get Botox injected directly into our eyes to keep us from weeping for our decadent, self-mutilating society.

"Toddlercore"[28]

"Toddlercore" is a school of fashion—first identified in 2014—in which adults dress like kids. Of course, Americans have been dressing like kids for years,[29] but we're not talking about sweatpants and T-shirts here. We're talking about grown-ups in pigtails wearing hooded onesies emblazoned with little pepperoni pizzas. For real. The term makes a lot of sense, since toddlers are humans between the ages of one and three, and that's also the number of minutes a rational adult can handle talking to another grown-up who clothes themselves this way.

"Hispandering"

Coined during the 2015–16 presidential campaign, "Hispandering" describes a political candidate's awkward attempts at appealing to Hispanic voters. An example might be a political candidate who, oh, we don't know, tweets a picture of himself eating a taco bowl on Cinco de Mayo.

Note: This term is not to be confused with "*hipster*andering," the act of manufacturing a food item, slapping a letterpressed label on it, and attempting to sell it for ten times its value.

Small Talk Type 3: Conceptual Art

Wherein you engage in the age-old argument: *Is* it conceptual art? Or is it trust fund kids entertaining themselves by doing outrageous things with other people's money? Discuss.

The Future Library

Artist Katie Paterson got the city of Oslo to fund an anthology of a hundred all-new books written by some of the world's great authors. The catch:

---

28   Note: Since "core" has become such a go-to suffix for modern portmanteaus (e.g., "normcore," "nerdcore"), we now declare the English language "core"-core.

29   We suspect that this tendency toward lazy, sloppy attire is partially grounded in America's growing addiction to another portmanteau: brunch.

The anthology won't be published until the year 2114. Between now and then, the books will be sealed, one per year, in a specially designed room in Oslo's Deichmanske Library, where they will be displayed but cannot be read. Meanwhile, a thousand trees have been planted for the sole purpose of providing the paper on which the books will be printed, a century from now.

Margaret Atwood contributed the first manuscript. We won't be alive to read it when the library opens, but we kind of hope it consists of a single word: "SUCKAHS."

Van Gogh's Ear

The story about van Gogh cutting off his ear? We've all heard it; that's not a good small talk story. The story about the Italian artist who *regrew* van Gogh's ear and put it in a museum where people can whisper into it? *That's* a good small talk story.

It's also true. Diemut Strebe obtained a tiny piece of Vincent van Gogh's brother's great-great-grandson's ear (with his permission, we hope). Thus it actually contains some of Vincent's DNA. Then Strebe recruited eggheads from MIT and Harvard to grow an ear out of it. It's made of "organic polymer"[30] and attached to machines to keep it "alive." The size and shape of the ear was calculated from the sole existing photograph depicting Vincent's head when it was still symmetrical.

Strebe has displayed the ear such that when people speak into it, they hear back something like white noise. We consider this a good metaphor for what happens to communication in a long-term relationship.

Everything

In 2012, the Dutch artist duo Lernert & Sander collected 1,400 samples of every perfume released that year, and poured them all into a 1.5-liter bottle.

---

30   Probably something like the stuff they make hot dogs out of.

They called the resulting fragrance/art installation "EVERYTHING." We call it "THE ALLERGY ATOM BOMB," capable of making everything in a two-mile radius smell like Macy's. God forbid it ever gets into the wrong hands.

(THE NEW) DON'Ts

We all know what society says we're not supposed to talk about at a dinner party. Religion. Politics. Our salaries. The fact that everybody occasionally[31] watches porn.[32]

In truth, we believe that all of these topics *are* fair game... just not till later, after the booze has taken hold (see chapter six, "Conversation").

In our opinion, though,

> Q: Why does Snoop Dogg carry an umbrella?
> A: Fo' drizzle.
> — CHARLAMAGNE THA GOD,
> RADIO STAR

there are *new* "don't"s: topics that have been creeping, kudzu-like, into modern dinner parties and strangling richer conversations, a.k.a. annoying us. Here are a few topics we'd be happy not to hear discussed at a party.

Transportation

The vehicular method by which you got to the party is boring. Likewise, the route you took and the challenges you faced along the way. Was traffic bad? Was it impossible to find parking? Was the L train down? Great. Here are some other facts: Water is wet, and Mom and Dad should get a divorce. These things are not news. The story about your excruciating journey, absent interesting characters or a surprising plot twist, is equally excruciating to listen to. And while certain government officials might say otherwise, torture is a crime.

---

31 Frequently.

32 Wait, you don't? Oh, us neither. Yeah, we were just joking around.

New TV Shows

Have you heard? TV has never been better! Yes, we *have* heard, because no one stops talking about it. Stop talking about it.

Also, stop telling us what happens in every episode of the show you're really into right now. Not because we fear spoilers. But because it's the twenty tens, and between Netflix, DVR, and YouTube, we can go home after the party and immediately start watching the show *for ourselves.* Hell, we can duck into the bathroom and start streaming it on our cell phones right now, *at this very party.* You may be a very good storyteller. We're betting the professionals who made the actual show are better.

Media-Created Narcissist of the Week

It's alarmingly easy for small talk to turn to the latest antics of reality TV stars, or Kim Kardashian–style celebutantes. To us, this is the conversational equivalent of inhaling secondhand smoke: It makes us sick, and we don't even get to look cool. Instead, please express outsize opinions about people who actually matter, like the head of the IMF, nuns in the world's poorest places, or public radio hosts with arbitrary opinions about what you should talk about.

Fecal Matters

Don't talk about poop.

SHOWING UP: GUIDELINES FOR GUESTS

Clearly, during the delicate Arrivals phase of a dinner party, much is expected of a host. But guests are not without responsibilities and expectations themselves. To wit:

1) SHOW UP ON TIME. ISH.

Do not be *too* on time. Fifteen or twenty minutes late is about right. This is because, as we've already noted, the host will likely not be ready for you. They will, at the last minute, suddenly remember they cleaned everything in the bathroom *except the toilet*. An ingredient will have been forgotten without which the roast will be sad and flavorless. Something will have fallen apart, like a flower vase, or their suddenly tantruming child. Give them a few extra minutes to take care of the problem…or to call in a panic asking *you* for help. Speaking of which:

2) BRING WHATEVER YOU'RE ASKED TO BRING.

In the hour preceding a dinner party, all guests become akin to volunteer firefighters: When an emergency call goes out from the host, everyone is required to heed it and bring to the party whatever is requested, be it ice, butter, or Ugandan hazelnut dust.

Occasionally, you'll encounter a host who abuses this power, requesting such items as a brand-new MacBook Air or a red-furred Shar-Pei with a lisp-bark. If so, sadly say that you'd *totally* do it, but you're in the car and about to arrive at the party any minute. When you finally show up a half hour later, blame traffic. After the party, delete the host from your phone/life.

3) PLUS A BOTTLE OF WINE.

If you are invited to a dinner party, regardless of what the host asks you to bring, you must also bring a bottle of wine. If you and a significant other have been invited, then you must *each* bring a bottle of wine. This prevents what was—before the advent of smartphones (see chapter one) — the biggest threat to a dinner party: running out of booze. Don't worry, the wine WILL be consumed. And if it isn't, well, you'll rarely hear a host mope about all the wine people gave them for free.

4) ENJOY YOURSELF.

Or at least *appear* to enjoy yourself. Example: You are part of a couple. On the way to the dinner party, you get in a screaming match. You think it's inappropriate of her to constantly "like" her ex's Instagram selfies, particularly since the dude is clearly just taking them from a high angle to hide the ham-and-cheese pouches that have sprung up along the jawline of his stupid fat aging face. She thinks you are being a freakish stalker, keeping obsessive track of her every social media move. You are allowed to bicker about this until you get to the host's front door. The second it opens, suck it up and smile. Note: As they say, "Fake it to make it." An hour into a good dinner party, you may find yourself smiling for real.

PART 4:
HISTORY LESSONS WITH BOOZE™

We conclude this chapter with the perfect fusion of Small Talk and Cocktails. Namely, compact historical anecdotes, designed to be discussed *with* an accompanying themed cocktail in hand.[33] It's what we cunningly call our History Lessons with Booze™.[34]

Oh, did we neglect to mention earlier that history is basically several millennia worth of great Small Talk fodder? Especially tales that fall into one of three categories. We list them below, with an example of each.

#1
THE ACCIDENT THAT MADE SOMEONE SUPER RICH

Inventor Lonnie Johnson will probably be remembered for the *least* important thing he ever made.

First, some background: Born in Mobile, Alabama, Lonnie took a quick interest in mechanics and science. He was the kind of kid who set the family kitchen on fire when he tried to whip up a batch of homemade rocket fuel.

Still, as an African American growing up in the segregated South, Lonnie wasn't encouraged to achieve much. But he did anyway, earning a master's in nuclear engineering. He went on to design circuitry for NASA's *Galileo* mission to Jupiter. He also worked on a little air force project called the stealth bomber.

But it was a humbler gadget that accidentally made Lonnie a fortune: a heat pump he designed in his spare time that used water instead of Freon. One day, when Lonnie was testing a prototype of the pump in his bathroom, the gizmo shot a powerful stream of water into the tub. His first thought: "This would make a great squirt gun!" He called it the Power Drencher.

---

33 Note: Because these cocktails were concocted by fancy professionals, they all require spirits in addition to the ones we listed previously. If you have neither the booze nor the cash to make them, just pair the histories with a martini.

34 This really is trademarked. We can technically sue you into poverty if you even say it aloud without paying a licensing fee. But as thanks for buying this book, we'll give you a pass.

The name didn't stick. But the toy did. Renamed the Super Soaker, it hit stores in 1989 and has since racked up around $2 billion in sales.

With the proceeds, Lonnie formed his own company. They're now working on an engine that would create solar power as efficiently as coal power, thereby saving the planet. Now if it also lets you drench your little brother from sixty feet away, they might be onto something.

❧ **THE MIDORI SOAKER** ❧

In honor of an excessively powerful squirt gun, here's a Southern variation on the excessively powerful Long Island iced tea, pumped up by Emi Bencsath of the Noble South, a bar in Lonnie Johnson's birthplace of Mobile, Alabama.

Ingredients:
3 peeled cucumber slices (about ¼ inch thick)
¼ ounce simple syrup
¾ ounce lime juice
¾ ounce Alabama's own 27 Springs gin
¾ ounce 27 Springs vodka
¾ ounce Bacardí white rum
⅓ ounce Yellow Chartreuse
¾ to 1 ounce Midori (depending on how sweet you want the drink)
4 sprigs mint
Chilled sparkling water

Directions:
In a cocktail shaker, muddle the cucumber slices with simple syrup. Add ice, Midori, vodka, gin, rum, Yellow Chartreuse, and lime juice. Shake the ingredients with the mint. Fill a pint glass three-quarters with fresh ice. Strain the drink into the glass and top with chilled sparkling water — preferably fired out of a bar gun.

THE POLITICIAN WITH A RIDICULOUS IDEA

Peter the Great tried to change the face of Russia. Literally.

It all began when Peter took a tour of Europe. In Holland, he learned shipbuilding. In Germany, he learned to wipe his lips with a dinner napkin. Peter fell in love with Western culture—surely *this* was the way of the future.

So when he got back home, Peter greeted his noblemen with a Western-style hug. Then he whipped out a razor... and cut off their beards. Western men were clean-shaven, he said, so Russians should be, too.

Problem was, Russians really dug their beards—aristocrats and the devoutly religious grew them down to their chests. So, to get everyone on board, Peter imposed a beard tax. You could keep your whiskers... if you paid the state one hundred rubles.

And once you paid, you had to carry around state-issued proof: a little coin stamped with a picture of a mustache and beard. Peter posted guards at city gates to make sure the unshaven had anted up. We are not making any of this up.

The beard tax never brought in much cash, and when Peter died, the tax went with him. But the war on beards continued elsewhere: Margaret Thatcher made every member of her cabinet shave. And Walt Disney outlawed beards for Disneyland workers—a ban that was only lifted in 2012. Animatronic Abe Lincoln is said to be pleased.

> ## ❧ THE RASPUTIN ❧
>
> As presented to us by Ken Biberaj, former vice president of the Russian Tea Room in New York City — where this drink was on the menu.
>
> *Ingredients:*
> 1 part Czar's Gold vodka
> 2 parts Frangelico
>
> *Directions:*
> In a cocktail shaker, combine the ingredients with ice. Shake and pour. Drink it quick. Pay the penalty: one hundred rubles (or local equivalent).

#3

THE DRINKING STORY

So there are drinking stories and then there are *drinking stories*. This is an example of the latter.

It was September 1956, and New Jersey resident Thomas Fitzpatrick was visiting pals in his old stomping grounds of Washington Heights, in New York City. After a few drinks at a bar, the story goes, someone proposed a bet: that Thomas couldn't get from Jersey to the Heights...in fifteen minutes.

Apparently, when he returned to Jersey that night, the challenge still stuck in his craw. So at around 3 a.m. he snuck into a single-engine plane at Teterboro School of Aeronautics. Then, fortified by the courage that had earned him a Purple Heart during the Korean War — and also maybe by beer — he flew the thing back to the Big Apple. Nailing a perfect landing on the street, right outside the bar.

In that gentler era, Thomas was hailed not as a threat to society but as a minor hero. The plane's owner refused to press charges. Instead of going to jail for grand larceny, Thomas received only a hundred-dollar fine as punishment.

Which might explain why, two years later, he did it *again*.

In October 1958, Thomas swiped *another* Teterboro plane, and flew it *again* to Washington Heights. Then he fled the scene, but he eventually gave himself up. Later, he told police he did it to prove to another bar patron that he'd actually done it the first time.

Not surprisingly, the judge threw the book at him. Thomas spent six months in jail—and then lived as a law-abiding citizen till his death in 2009. His obituary does not specify how much cash he won in the bet.

❧ THE LATE-NIGHT FLIGHT ❧

As assembled for us by Danny Beason of New Leaf, a restaurant in the Manhattan neighborhood that Fitzpatrick twice used as a runway.

Ingredients:
½ ounce Kahlúa
1½ ounces vodka
½ ounce Chambord
5 blackberries
1 egg white
Dash simple syrup

Directions:
The idea here is to create a layered representation of NYC's nighttime sky.

Pour earthen-colored Kahlúa into the base of a cocktail glass.

In a separate mixing glass, muddle the blackberries, add Chambord and one ounce of vodka, and shake with ice. Hold the bowl of a spoon, back side up, very close to the surface of the Kahlúa, and strain the dark-purplish Chambord mixture slowly and carefully over it, creating a second layer.

In another mixing glass, shake the egg white, syrup, and remaining half ounce of vodka — without ice — to create an emulsion. Layer this fluffy white foam on top, like the clouds through which Mr. Fitzpatrick piloted.

Sip and enjoy, preferably far from any enticing airfields.

CHAPTER FIVE

THE MAIN COURSE

You're an hour or so into your party. The cocktails have taken effect, a base coat of appetizer has been applied to everyone's stomachs, people are getting nice and chatty, and you're ready to put dinner on the table. This is a good time for us to talk about the least important part of a dinner party: the food.

It's okay to go back and read that sentence a second time; we know you think you misread it. Or better yet, we'll say it again for emphasis, using italics: *The food is the least important part of a dinner party.*

Yes, a dinner party must occur over dinner. Yes, we have specifically said that you need to have cooked the bare majority of the dinner yourself. But reader, this is for *purely metaphorical reasons.*

Giving homemade food to your guests is a metaphor for sharing and openness. Gathering around a dinner table to consume it is a metaphor for community. Eating it in unison is a metaphor for mutual understanding. And you'll be evoking these metaphors even if your baked salmon is overcooked. Or if you burned it and had to serve toast and water instead. The food is only there to get people to chill together.

Now, this is not to say you should serve your guests gruel. You are a good/sane enough person not to plan a menu which consists of a bowl of unpeeled onions. Your food must be palatable and nonpoisonous and demonstrate that you put in a modicum of effort. But anything beyond that is gravy.[1]

Of course, you might still want some tips for planning a menu. Or for avoiding potential pitfalls, as you cook and serve various foodstuffs. Most importantly, during our years as Associate Fellows of Applied Levity in the College of Celebratory Sciences[2] at Cambridge University, we took note of a few strategies and rules of etiquette that will make for a happier party *while* you eat. All of this we outline for you below, hooray.

PART 1: MAKING THE FOOD

Just to be clear? We really really really like food. In fact, obtaining free food is more than half the reason we got into this racket. It's also why Rico no longer fits into any of the pants he owned when we launched the show.

And hey, perhaps you're a food hobbyist who wants to go all out for your guests. You know the difference between millet and a mullet, and you want to show it. You know that black tea steeps perfectly in 198-degree water, and that chickens taste better when they were raised listening to Haydn. If that's you, you are welcome to make a fancy meal. But we suspect if you're that person, you're also probably skipping over the "food" section of this book. For the rest of the world, here's a guide to putting food on the dinner party table.

SELECTING A MENU

1. Cookbooks

Many novice party throwers will turn to cookbooks for ideas about what to cook. There are three types of cookbooks. For the novice party thrower, we recommend none of them.

The first and most typical kind are trade paperbacks with pastel-colored

1 Including, often, actual gravy. Gravyless chicken, for instance, is fine.
2 Does not exist. Working on it.

titles printed on a white cover. They comprise half the book section at your local Goodwill and were all written between 1979 and 1995. Many refer to pasta as a diet food. Avoid.

The second kind—found conspicuously close to the art books at Barnes & Noble—consist of twenty actual recipes, fattened up with hundreds of color-saturated photographs of perfectly art-directed roasts and legumes. These are bound together into a gorgeous hardbound tome you'd never want to bring into an actual kitchen, for fear of soiling the pages' coarse matte finish. These cookbooks aren't for cooking. They are for gift giving and for building booster seats for toddlers.

Third are what we call the "finger crusher" cookbooks. Volumes so enormous that if one accidentally slammed shut on your hand, it would mash your bones to powder.[3] Recently, we calculated the average number of ingredients in a finger crusher cookbook recipe, and that number was 1,748. Like most utopian fantasies, the dishes in there sure seem amazing (maple-glazed dove kidneys with caterpillar eyelashes and shark mucosa; tickled Brussels sprouts with Tasmanian book dust and thirty-day-aged otter hips) but in truth could never be realized without the help of an army of slaves—er, "line cooks." If you do decide to cook from one of these cookbooks, we suggest you approach your local credit union for a small business loan, and begin cooking at least four months in advance of your party. Also, buy a box of pasta and a jar of sauce. That way your partner can whip something up for your guests before they take a group trip to visit you at the sanitarium.

2. Magazines/Newspapers/Food Websites

Every day, our friends in food media ticker-tape the world with a forest's worth of publications filled with seductive recipes. Often, they are accompanied by photographs of people just *slightly* more attractive than you and

---

3   For instance, Alain Ducasse's aptly titled, thousand-page, twelve-pound *Grand Livre de Cuisine*, available on Amazon for a mere $500.

your friends, enjoying what seem to be humble meals they made all on their lonesome. The headlines prominently feature variations on the words "simple," "easy," "quick," and "fun." Gosh, who wouldn't want to try to cook some new thing that's simple, easy, quick, and fun? Answer: You and your fragile nervous system, the day of a dinner party.

This is neither the time nor the venue for tackling an untried recipe, straightforward though it may seem. As with a new romance, once you're in the thick of a recipe, what started out breezy and awesome can quickly turn harsh and bleak, *for no reason at all*. Those smiling people in the food magazines are *models*. They were *paid* to smile.

If you insist on being adventurous, fine: try a new appetizer or side dish. But prepare it twice before the night of your gathering. Not only will you have the recipe down, but you'll be totally sick of it by the time you serve it, leaving more for your guests to enjoy while you down another drink.

3. Personal Repertoire

Now we're talking. As when writing a first novel, for a first dinner party we recommend you cook up something you know: a dish you've cooked for years and can pull off with a reasonable expectation of not setting yourself or anyone else ablaze.

What's that? You don't *have* any dishes in your personal repertoire? In that case, go back in time and redo your young adulthood.[4] Within a few years of leaving the family womb, an adult Homo sapiens ought to know how to prepare a few basic meals—and we're sorry, "Top ramen with onion dip" does not count as one of them.

You should master the quick preparation of at least four dishes: a "put calories in your body before you pass out" meal like spaghetti carbonara; an "unexpected visitors" meal like pork chops and salad; a "cook-to-impress

---

4   Actually, we're not total jerks: for novices we've scattered recipes for a foolproof dinner party menu throughout this section. Sorry if we were brusque just then. We were hangry.

date night dinner" like cocoa-dipped deep-fried oysters...and the thing you're gonna cook for your party—the Group Meal. A.k.a. a giant bowl of pasta or a platterful of something large you've roasted.

Under no circumstance should you attempt to simply make a quadruple portion of your "date night" meal! It will not be easy to scale up, and it will not result in the orgy you secretly desire.

FOOD BASICS

Regardless of whether you are drawing from a recipe or your intuition, take a moment to review the basics of each dinner party food type and how to deploy them properly.

Bread

Bread has taken a beating in the press in recent years, because it contains calories, sickens celiacs, and who knows, probably deals arms in eastern Africa. Nonetheless, WE EMBRACE IT. Bread is the stuff of life, the cornerstone of civilization, the gluten in "gluteus." *It's time to stop the bread hate.* Bread is two-thirds of sandwiches, 97 percent of buttered toast, and 100 percent within someone's power to not eat too much of.[5]

Also, thanks to the gutting of well-paying factory jobs and the stagnant wages/stifling atmosphere of office work, more and more people have resorted to opening local bakeries—thus making *actual* bread available where once you could buy only a plastic sock filled with slices of Nerf. There has never been a better time in America to be a bread eater!

This is great news, because bread is the most versatile of foods. It serves as a little edible plate for appetizers. It fills the stomach of vegetarians when hosts forget to make salad (see this chapter, "Make a Salad"). And it acts as Mother Nature's Swiffer, cleaning your plate of all its drippings.

---

5   Also, the classic shorthand phrase for "dinner party" is "breaking bread." What would we call it if we rid dinner parties of bread? "Breaking seaweed sheets"?

Yes, the two of you with celiac disease should not eat bread. (See this chapter, "Don't Make People Sick or Dead.") But to those who've abandoned bread for love handle reasons, we suggest you take the *Dinner Party Download* Carbo-Offset Pledge™: For each slice of bread you eat at a dinner party, you vow to replace a future slice of toast with a piece of romaine lettuce. This will not only even out your calorie intake, you'll lose water weight from the tears you'll shed looking back on the days when your metabolism actually metabolized things.

Notes on Presentation:

Don't tell our therapists, but we think a whole baguette is a beautiful thing. Ripping off chunks from it is the punk thing to do, but if you must cut it, don't slice the whole deal into little bread coins and toss it in a basket, where it will lose its rustic grandeur and quickly go stale. Instead, tear the loaf in half, set one piece aside, rip the second part into hunks, and place it all on a cutting board.

Serve non-baguettes on a cutting board, too, alongside a big-ass knife because it looks cool and tough — the food equivalent of a biker gang.

If you're thinking of putting a bag of sliced bread on the dinner table, please return this book to the retailer whence it was purchased and say to the clerk, "Please kill me." Or reread chapter one, where we told you to take food out of its packaging, hoss.

Meat

We are big fans of serving a big, dramatic piece of meat, a.k.a. "stunt meat." That means a leg of lamb, or a whole roasted chicken, or a big old "joint," as the Brits call it.[6] Meat that looks like it could appear at a dinner party in a cartoon is what you're going for.

A big hunk of charred meat has much to recommend it. It's super easy to cook. (The hardest part is forking over the not-small sum of money required

---

6   For a discussion of American joints, see chapter seven.

to get non-hormone-addled meat, but after that you just need to season it, pop it in the oven, and drink till your timer goes "beep.") It looks really impressive. (A large piece of charred mammal strums some primal chord in the human eater, so that even some of you vegetarians are tempted—you know you are.) And last, it's certain to feed your guests *and* provide enough leftovers to sustain you while you're cleaning your house for the next month. We recommend a roast bigger than a sneaker and smaller than a cargo van.

Notes on Presentation:

Roast meat needs to "rest" for a bit after being cooked, so the juices don't all spill out when you slice it. Perhaps it's this penchant for napping that endears it to our hearts. Anyway, while it does, place it at the center of your table. This lets guests know that feasting time is nigh, and that you obviously spent a lot of goddamn money on this party—so they should keep their complaints to a minimum.

ROAST CHICKEN

Buy the nicest 3½-to-4-pound chicken you can find.[7]

Salt and pepper the chicken inside and out.

Preheat the oven to 400 degrees.

Cut up an onion and stick it inside the chicken.

Stick whatever herbs you have on hand inside.

Slather the bird in olive oil and place it in a skillet.

Roast for twenty minutes breast side up, then flip.

Roast for another twenty minutes, then flip.

Roast for ten to twenty minutes, until a thermometer tells you the meat's reached 160 degrees, then...

Let it rest for five to ten minutes, and carve.

---

7   Note: Try not to skimp on the meat! Not only for environmental, ethical, and health reasons, but because bourgeois chickens straight-up taste better.

Seafood

Seafood should only be on your menu if you are a moderately advanced or advanced chef. This is because seafood is easy to overcook, can sicken guests if it's undercooked, and can make your house smell like a laundry hamper in an MMA locker room.

When preparing a menu around seafood, keep in mind that in many cases, once the bones and/or shells are removed, there will be about half an ounce of edible meat per guest. That's fine, since seafood is the one type of food you DO NOT want to serve in overabundance. The goal is to have NO LEFTOVERS. Seafood doesn't keep long, and if you throw it in the garbage, you're basically creating a rotting-fish potpourri. So prepare just enough for your guests to COMPLETELY CONSUME. You won't need a lot anyway, because although some (us included) consider sea creatures the ultimate luxury food, a goodly portion of Americans have it tied with colonoscopies as their least favorite thing.

Notes on Presentation:

Since there is so little fish in most fish, seek out big, meaty varieties like salmon. Then approximate the drama of "stunt meat" by serving it whole. Fillet it into portions before placing it on the table, though—otherwise, as guests stab into it, it'll shred into a pile of fish flakes.

Also bring out a bowl for discarded fish bones. Fun game: When you remove the bone-filled bowl post-meal, look any non-celiac Gluten Avoiders dead in the eye and intone, "*This* is what you're going to look like if you continue to avoid bread."

Lasagna, Paella, and Other Alpha Dishes

If you're not going with a hunk of meat or fish for your main course, select an "alpha dish"—something big and rich that at least looks like it took a lot of work. This should be something that completely fills your biggest pan or bowl. Lasagna is a popular alpha dish, as is paella.

Be aware, however, that alphas were invented in an era before dual-income families worked twenty-seven-hour days. An era before the invention of apps that allow you to order osso buco tacos with a pinky-tap. In other words: an era when people had *patience* and *time*. Hence these dishes can take a thousand hours to make. Cook them if you have social anxiety and don't want to interact with your guests for the first half of the evening.

Notes on Presentation:
The ideal presentation for an alpha dish is on Instagram.

Vegetables

Time was when vegetables were a frozen greenish brick you placed in a bowl, microwaved, and served covered in butter. Now there are root vegetable moussakas and roasted cauliflower steaks. In many quarters, all-veggie meals are deservedly the rage. Eggplant parm is the new chicken parm.

And yet—speaking of rage—if you live in a region where the economy is based on pig or cattle ranching, you should let your guests know in advance that you're planning to go the veggie route. Otherwise they will show up expecting cooked flesh, and are likely to snap and tear into your dog's Snausages for a meat fix. Know also that in parts of Spain, serving a meal without a pork product is still grounds for war.

Indeed, we fear it will take years for all-vegetable meals to be considered fully acceptable in all areas of the world. Veggies have too long a history as mere side dishes. As with Brooklyn or Camilla Parker-Bowles, it can take a long time for a support act to become a headliner.

That said, we encourage you to embrace the vegetable revolution. If nothing else, it involves 100 percent less killing than meat, is a helluva lot cheaper, and can be way kinder to your health. However, in a dinner party context, we advise making your vegetables as tasty as possible by making them as unhealthy as possible.[8] Cover them with salt, slather them in butter or oil, or add meat.

Notes on Presentation:

If veggies are the main dish, own it: give them pride of place at the center of the table.

Toss and dress salads BEFORE heading to the table, because a) this isn't an Outback Steakhouse salad bar, where people get to choose, and b) mixing a salad at a crowded dinner table is certain to end in at least one accidental bloody nose.

ARUGULA SALAD WITH AVOCADO

2 five-ounce containers arugula

1 shallot

1 medium avocado

⅓ cup pepitas (raw or salted)

2 tablespoons olive oil

⅔ tablespoon apple cider vinegar

Salt and pepper

Rinse the arugula, pat or spin it dry, and place it in a bowl.

Cut the circumference of the avocado lengthwise and split it in two around the pit. Gently pull apart the avocado and remove the pit.

Run a butter knife gently between the meat in each half of the avocado and the skin, then score the meat and scoop the now minced avocado bits into the bowl with the arugula.

Mince a tablespoon of shallot and add it to the bowl.

Pour the olive oil and vinegar into the salad.

Toss and add salt and pepper to taste.

---

8   See peperonata recipe, chapter three.

Starch

Unless your entree is an alpha dish that involves pasta, potatoes, or rice, you'll be serving one of those starches as a side. Grains, beans, and legumes all qualify, too. Aside from offering essential nutrients and being a delicious way to absorb the savory nectar that leaks from your entrée, starch is inexpensive and can help fill out a meal in the event that, say, the prime rib has shrunk, during cooking, into a subprime rib. Starch also provides basic sustenance to the picky eater who's been surreptitiously feeding their asparagus spears to the dog all night.

Notes on Presentation:

Since starches generally come in various shades of white or beige, served alone they can appear bland. Throwing some parsley on top can help, but really the best idea is to get starches out of their serving vessel and in close proximity to the vivid hues of the entrée's meat-and-sauce juice as quickly as possible.

SHORT-GRAIN BROWN RICE

1 cup brown rice
1¾ cups water

Combine the rice and water in a small pot with a lid, bring to a boil, then reduce to a light simmer for around forty minutes.
If the rice is too chewy for you, add an additional ounce or two of water and continue simmering.
Remove from the heat and add a pat of good butter and salt.

Dessert

As much as it pains us to say it, dessert is a must for a dinner party. It pains us because we are not huge dessert people. But dinner parties call for a sense of occasion. And we grudgingly admit that nothing does that better than punctuating your meal with a big pile of sugarfat.

Since baking is time-consuming and can require OCD-level attention to detail, baked goods are the sole food items we actually encourage hosts to purchase premade and/or subcontract out to another guest. Barring that, we ourselves have a taste for easy-to-prepare fruit, cheese, and nuts plates. Alas, for many Americans, that's not dessert; it's a snack at your office desk.

In other words, let them eat cake. Or chocolate (see sidebar).

Notes on Presentation:

Serve dessert after the table is entirely clear of the savory dishes that came before. This process also acts as an intermission during which guests can use the facilities, sneak a cigarette, or pretend they forgot something in the car and go obsessively check their social media. When people return to the party, they find the table emptied of sullied dishes, with dessert front and center. How delightful!

A special note regarding ice cream: Before serving, you'll want to remove it from the freezer to let it thaw a bit, so that it comes out in nice ball-shaped scoops. Note also that there is a 99 percent chance you will forget you did this, and by the time you remember, the ice cream will have melted into a gluey soup that is seeping out of its cardboard container all over your kitchen counter. Therefore, a suggestion: Don't serve ice cream.

 TWO FANCY-ASS CHOCOLATE BARS

2 fancy-ass chocolate bars

Break the chocolate into asymmetrical bits while still in the wrapper.
Serve by unwrapping the chocolate at the table and leaving the bits on top of the fancy-ass packaging.

PART 2: CONSUMING THE FOOD

In the "etiquette" segment of our show, we and a rotating cast of celebrities answer our listeners' questions about how to behave. Roughly three-quarters of these concern the politest way to serve, eat, and otherwise be civil around food.

On what side of the plate does the steak knife go? Must one really tip the bowl away from one's body as one scoops up the last spoonful of soup? What if I don't like Brussels sprouts? If they're on the table, must I eat them anyway? And must I really put the *s* after "Brussel" in "Brussels sprouts"?

Once again, the thing to keep in mind here is NOBODY CARES. Even if your guests *know* what side the fork's supposed to go on, they're not going to judge you on its placement. If you don't like Brussels[9] sprouts, just put a token few on your plate and forget to eat them. By this point in the evening most of the guests will be too lit to notice anyway.

Nonetheless, we acknowledge there are some situations, unique to the consumption of food at dinner parties, which the novice host may find challenging to navigate politely. Here are some guidelines.

❧ ❧ ❧

"Never admit a mistake! I've learned that from one of the people that are running for president this year: Never admit a mistake. So, if you have a little bit of food, and some accidentally, as it often will, flips from the tip of your tongue onto the cheek of your compadre... simply chew a big bunch of food, and spit it all over his face. Double down. And then just keep talking."
— NORM MACDONALD, 2016

❧ ❧ ❧

---

9   *Or* "Brussel." In conversation no one can hear the difference.

This isn't a wedding. Or the Nobel Prize ceremony. You needn't assemble a seating chart to take into account every possible vector of conversation, or each guest's current status in your peer group's social hierarchy. These people are grown-ups—you can let them choose where to sit for dinner. With a few exceptions.

1. The Odd-Man-Out Exception

Suppose you've got a roomful of guests who are all old friends, except one guy: Ned. As everyone seats themselves, Ned hangs back, unsure of where to insert himself around the table. You *invited* poor Ned; cheerily tell him to sit next to you.

2. The Bestie Exception

You've been working hard all day to put your party together. For the last hour, you've been zipping from person to person, making sure everyone's liquored up and happy. The one chance you'll have to spend quality time with your best friend Nance is if you seat her next to you during dinner. So seat Nance next to you during dinner—you deserve it! Put her on the side not being occupied by Ned.

3. The Throw-Yourself-on-the-Grenade Exception

Wilberly, the underwear model you met at a coffee shop yesterday and invited to your party on a whim, turns out to be an ass when drunk. He has been uncomfortably hitting on your pal Lucinda since his first vodka soda. As you all sit down for dinner, he is making a lecherous beeline for the seat beside her. It is now your duty to say, through gritted teeth, "Come sit next to *me*, Wilberly," gesturing to the seat beside you that is as far from Lucinda as possible.

Note: *This rule supersedes the Bestie Exception*. Meaning you must displace your bestie with Wilberly, and heroically doom yourself to an evening of enduring his insensitive jokes. Lucinda will repay you with everlasting gratitude and by forgiving you for inviting Wilberly in the first place.

4. The Insufferable Couple Exception

Belle and Biff just got back from their honeymoon! Oh my God, Belize was *amazing!* And they literally *cannot stop talking about it! FOR EVEN A SECOND!!!* Break the cycle: Seat Belle and Biff far away from each other.

Of course, keep in mind that to prevent this move from looking conspicuous, you'll also need to split up any other couples. We know: annoying. For this reason, do not invite newlyweds to your dinner party until three to six months after their wedding.

FOOD PREFERENCES/DIETS

It is our contention that a dinner party, like Thanksgiving dinner, is an Official Food Immunity Zone™, a special occasion during which you should serve — and your guests should be encouraged to eat — whatever you like, diets be damned. Just keep two things in mind.

1. Make a salad.

When you decide to throw a dinner party, assume you're making a salad. It's nice and healthy. But you may also need something to serve Vegan Vicki, who waited till now to tell you she's vegan.

Note: You are not doing this to make Vegan Vicki happy. As outlined in chapter two, Vegan Vicki was supposed to tell you about her dietary needs the second she accepted your invitation, and she was supposed to offer to bring her own damned vegan dish.

No, you're doing this for the benefit of the *rest* of your guests, so they don't feel guilty chowing down on pork tenderloin while Vegan Vicki sits glumly in front of her empty plate, getting angry-drunk on her empty stomach.

2. Don't make people sick or dead.

Nothing will ruin your reputation as a host faster than having a guest vomit or die at the dinner table. Yet a surprising number of people *really* don't want to take this rule seriously.

We have met chefs who on some level, for instance, don't believe anyone really suffers from celiac disease. In fact, around half a million Americans are certified celiacs. True, in a country of five hundred million, that's not a huge percentage. You may be right to suspect that the self-diagnosed "celiac" at your party is just a fad dieter who avoids gluten because that's what Victoria Beckham is doing. But don't find out you're wrong by sneaking wheat into their food and making them pop like a balloon.

Similarly, if a guest warns you that they have, say, a severe nut allergy, play it safe and don't put *anything* with nuts *anywhere near* the table. There comes a point at a dinner party when tipsy guests will aimlessly bite into anything that looks salty. You don't want Allergy Joe's throat to swell shut because he accidentally nibbled one of your Peanut Butter Pecan–Almond Soybean clusters.

THE LAST PIECE

It's the eternal question of dining etiquette: Assuming everyone at the table has had an equal portion of food, who gets the last piece remaining on a communal serving dish?

In our experience, this conundrum is typically solved via one of three methods, all of them lame.

a) MUTUAL PASSIVITY: *No one* takes it. The final chicken wing, dumpling, nacho chip, or pizza slice sits there until it rots—the sacrificial morsel which symbolically allows all assembled to quietly assure themselves they are not, in fact, gluttonous barbarians.

b) INFINITE DIVISION (a.k.a. "hippie halves"): This involves each guest cutting off a small portion of the last bit of food, until a fragment so tiny remains that it becomes subject to the laws of quantum physics. This is both ridiculous and mutually destructive: Rather than allow a single guest to get a satisfying final portion, the group silently works together to guarantee they *all* get a deeply *un*satisfying one. And when it's all over, there's *still* a little piece of food sitting there.

c) THE ALPHA INTERVENTION: An "Alpha" guest boldly declares he or she will take the last piece...that is, "as long as no one else wants it." For someone to now lay claim to the piece would involve rudely justifying why they deserve it more than anyone else. Therefore, the Alpha is not only allowed but *encouraged* by the group to take the piece.

Though this seems like a decent outcome — the piece is fully consumed and the group is rid of the anxiety it causes — the Alpha is always left feeling selfish, and everyone else is left feeling steamrolled.

Therefore, we support a FOURTH, BEST solution: You, the host, should decide and announce to whom the final piece should be awarded. Here are some possible rationales on which to base your decision.

1. The Meritorious Service Award

One of your guests volunteered to painstakingly shuck three dozen clams for your turkey stuffing. Or they talked your upstairs neighbor out of calling in a noise complaint. Or they were *unable* to talk the neighbor out of calling in a noise complaint, but made up for it by bribing the cops when they showed up. For this, said guest deserves the last piece.

2. The Congratulatory Award

A guest at your dinner table recently birthed a child, celebrated a birthday, got a promotion, or had sex with someone who — all assembled agree — is an extremely enviable person with whom to have had sex. By way of congratulations, award this guest the final piece.

3. The "That Was Classic" Award

Perhaps a guest brought, as their contribution to the meal, a single white truffle worth $10,000. Or perhaps they tripped on the way up the steps to your house, banged their skull into the railing, and arrived at your door with a bleeding head wound that is still oozing an hour later. Either way, they contributed something spectacular that no one in attendance will soon forget. For this the guest deserves the final piece and, if needed, a ride to the emergency room.

4. The Bottomless Stomach Award

There is generally one person at a dinner party who is known for quickly and proudly pounding down unholy amounts of food. This person is usually infuriatingly thin, and totally comfortable with his reputation as a glutton. Awarding this person the final piece makes everyone happy: He gets food, and the others get to gently mock him — the only socially acceptable way to express their jealousy of his supernatural genetics.

5. The Mathematical Method

If you prefer an objectively fair, data-driven method for determining the taker of the final piece, simply assign each guest a number "X" by applying the formula

$$X = A+B^2-(0+Z)-Q^2$$

in which

> A = the number of bottles of wine the guest brought
> B = the number of days before the party the guest finally deigned to RSVP
> 0 = represents the time the *first* guest arrived at the party
> Z = the number of minutes later *this* guest arrived at the party
> Q = the number of times the guest checked his/her smartphone during dinner.

The guest with the highest number is awarded the final piece.

Example:
Sholanda RSVP'd seven days ago, brought two bottles of wine, showed up first, and switched off her smartphone as soon as she arrived. We would mathematically represent her thusly:

$$2+7^2-(0+0)-0^2 = \textbf{51}$$

Meanwhile, Jedediah showed up without RSVP'ing at all, forgot to bring wine, arrived sixty-eight minutes after Sholanda, and sent ten texts before dessert was even served. We express him, numerically, like so:

$$0+0^2-(0+68)-10^2 = \textbf{negative 168}$$

Clearly, in this scenario, Sholanda gets the final piece. Jedediah gets a punch in the mouth.

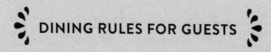

DINING RULES FOR GUESTS

Guests, here's a brief guide to what's expected from *you* at the dinner party table in return for your free meal.

1) TAKE ONE BITE, FOR GOD'S SAKE

So we understand you are not a fan of Brussels sprouts. Yet the host has proudly placed a tureen of them before you. Unless you have a good medical reason not to, be a grown-up, put some on your plate, and take a bite of them anyway.[10] To do otherwise is to disdain the host's labor and, as Anthony Bourdain advised us, possibly their entire freaking family.

2) COMPLIMENT

The food the host cooked for you this evening is going to be great. How do we know? *Because you are going to say so.* Even if the food, in fact, sucks.

Our rule of thumb: Within five minutes of the meal being served, someone at the table MUST thank and compliment the chef. If that person is not you, your contribution is to nod your head in vigorous agreement and murmur appreciatively.

Be aware that at this moment, it is customary for the host to shyly apologize for aspects of the meal that were not up to their own exacting standards. In almost all cases,[11] *you are to tell the host the food is excellent and they are being ridiculous.* The French fries are *delicious* once you scrape off the burned parts! You think putting

---

10 You don't have to finish them, because another grown-up thing for guests to do is not comment on whether another guest has cleaned their plate.

11 Exception: If you suspect the food may be actually dangerous. The chicken is cold and raw inside? Gently suggest it could use a few more minutes in the oven. Your right to life trumps the host's right to gratitude.

marshmallows on the flatbread was a *great* idea! Your *favorite kind of salad* is a few leaves of iceberg lettuce wilting in a pool of sunflower oil! Has your host ever thought about opening a restaurant?

3) TAKE A SECOND HELPING

It's perfectly okay to take a second helping of food. This is because, as a polite guest, you took a pathetically small *first* helping. You know this, right? When the communal entrée is first passed to you, your job is to gauge the amount of it you'd *like* to have...and take *half* that much. Once everyone has been served, *then* you're allowed a second helping, three to ten times as large as the first.

4) KEEP YOUR NAPKIN ON YOUR LAP

a) Because by the end of the meal, a napkin becomes so streaked with various foodstuffs it resembles a discarded field dressing on a World War I battlefield. You want it out of sight.

b) Because tucking it into the neck of your shirt makes you look like a cross between a seventeenth-century fop and a guy from a vaguely racist spaghetti sauce commercial circa 1975.

c) To signal you're not leaving the table anytime soon. Indeed, the universally agreed-upon signal that the meal is about to *end* is when guests take the napkins from their laps and toss them back on the table, like a boxing coach lobbing a towel of surrender into the ring.

✦ ✦ ✦

*"You have disrespected your host, okay? You've
rejected a beloved dish that's reflective of probably
personal history. That tripe à la mode could be a
beloved family dish. You just basically spat in the
milk of their mother. You rejected any possibility
of trying something new. You revealed yourself
to be an inward-looking buffoon and no one
I would want to be friends with.
"Look, take a little bite. Just try a little bite. If you don't
like [it], say, 'Not really to my taste.' That is a respectable
response. Just try a little bit."*

— ANTHONY BOURDAIN

✦ ✦ ✦

CHAPTER SIX

CONVERSATION

Dinner is served, small talk has been exchanged, ice has been broken. You've moved on from the giddy buzz of cocktails to the mellow joy of wine. You and your guest are vibing as one. Now, as you eat, comes the part of the party where you *really* change the world.

It's called "deep conversation"—a.k.a. what civilized people do when they're not voting, giving money to public radio, or fantasizing about having kinky yet respectful sex. And speaking of civilization, if you've followed our instructions thus far, what you've done is create a miniature version thereof: You've lured all different kinds of folks into your dining room with the promise of sustenance, they've agreed to sit down peacefully and to behave with some amount of decorum, and now you're all going to talk about everything that's wrong and right with the world. It's kind of like a UN summit, if the agenda included both Middle East crisis management *and* the social value of superhero movies. And if a couple of diplomats made out in the bathroom.[1]

This is what dinner parties are for: The lively exchange of ideas, plus food and booze. It's the most sensual setting for potentially groundbreaking debate and mutual discovery ever invented. If you do this correctly,

---

1   Not being UN representatives ourselves, though, we can't say with certainty that this *doesn't* happen at summits, like, all the time.

everyone will end the evening enriched, they'll go on to throw their own dinner parties, and so on and so on until society is saved from all the damage wrought by brunch.

It seems like conversing over dinner would be an easy thing for a modern human being to do. After all, you've been exposed to dinner table conversations since you were old enough to sit in a high chair without Mom's hand on your neck to support your giant baby cranium.

Or *have* you? The sad fact is, fewer and fewer American families regularly eat meals together,[2] meaning millions have grown up *deprived* of dinner table conversations. We can't help but suppose decades of this has brought us to the current sad state of affairs—whereby people feel compelled to read a book authored by two strangers from the radio just for advice about talking to other people.

The good news: We have written that book, and you hold it in your hands! Read on for some easy guidelines regarding making Big Talk…as well as strategies for dealing with those at your party who want to do all the talking for everybody.

PART 1: RULES OF ENGAGEMENT

A.K.A. THE EIGHT ESSENTIAL RULES OF CONVERSATION, COURTESY OF TWO PROFESSIONAL BLABBERMOUTHS

Confession: We don't have dinner parties every day. To be honest, most nights are a tray of store-bought hummus, public radio on low, and tears.

---

2   Which is too bad, since, according to a 2015 article in the *Washington Post,* kids who dine with their families have better vocabularies, get higher scores on achievement tests, and are less prone to smoking or teen pregnancy. Seriously. Also, we heard they are more likely to be able to levitate and to turn pollution into delicious cookies.

But here *is* something we do most days: talk to people.

In fact, we've made careers out of talking to people. We know, we can't believe it either.[34] Parades of interviewees come by to chat, and we're expected to pull interesting conversations out of them. We need to get them talking, whether or not they want to. We need them to sound smart and engaging, whether or not they are. We need $2 million each, a pair of crimson Alfa Romeo Spiders, and people who love us even though we snore.

But we digress. The point is: During our almost-decade in the talk radio trenches, we have gleaned a set of conversational rules that may not *guarantee* sparkling repartee…but can certainly increase the likelihood it will occur. And these rules work for anyone! Even if you didn't grow up a bird-chested asthmatic who had to learn, at a young age, how to charm bullies in order to avoid finding yourself on the wrong end of a knuckle croissant. Although that helps.

RULE 1: SHUT UP

The secret to conversation starting really boils down to this:

No one cares what *you* have to say; they care about what THEY have to say.

Our friends at the public radio show *StoryCorps* put a more positive spin on this: "Listening," they say, "is an Act of Love." Hippies.

But they're right — ask any therapist. Deep down, what folks want more than their mother in a wedding dress is to feel they've been *heard*. And the best way to engender that feeling is to let them talk. Which they can't do if *you* are talking. Therefore, when in doubt, *be quiet* and *listen*. This

---

3   To our fourth-grade teachers: See? We CAN talk incessantly and still be productive members of society! Also, it was Brendan who put peanut butter in Stefanie Sewell's social studies book. But she started it.

4   We have also, as noted in an earlier chapter, made careers out of eating weird things. Which Rico's mom finds particularly amusing given that she spent most of his childhood trying to convince him to eat something other than spaghetti and fried chicken. No, not together.

is a win-win, because listening not only makes guests feel appreciated, it also allows you to use your mouth for other things, like guzzling down a second helping of scalloped potatoes.

We know this isn't as easy as it sounds. If you're throwing a dinner party, you're probably a social person who likes to share with other people. You *like* to talk. We ourselves don't shut up nearly as much as we should, but since we do a pretaped radio show, we have the advantage of being able to edit out a lot of the stupid things we say. Also, since we're on the radio, we don't have to wear pants. Neither of these things will work well when hosting a dinner party. When hosting a dinner party, you should always try to shut up, and you should almost always wear pants.

RULE 2: TO EXTRACT A STORY, GO TO EXTREMES

Of course, part of listening does involve some talking…in controlled bursts we in the industry call "questions."

The goal of asking questions is to get guests to abandon the Small Talk we were all making earlier and get them to share the important, insightful, or hilarious things that reside in their brainpan. Often in the form of a story.

Stories are how humans best process information and ideas.[5] In fact, actor and writer Alan Alda told us that storytelling essentially allows human beings to mind meld.

> "Well, what [stories] do—according to scientists I have
> interviewed who use functional MRIs to study the
> storytelling encounter—is they actually seem to sync
> up the brain in a real way. The brain of the person

---

5   They are also a natural resource being strip-mined by media outlets like the Moth and countless podcasts. A recent report from the National Story Defense Council claims we've reached "peak story," and that at this rate the story supply will be exhausted by 2027. Actually, that'd make a great story.

telling the story...when he tells it to someone else, *her* brain lights up or is activated in a very similar way to *his* brain as he tells the story. I think you could say we synchronize through stories."

In other words, according to Hawkeye, when we read Zadie Smith, her brain touches ours. Ironically, when we realized that, we lost our minds.

Now, some guests will be natural storytellers—the type who can spontaneously spin compelling yarns about, like, shoe shopping. But others need their long-dormant storytelling gene activated. And we've found that one quick way to do it is to *ask them questions about extremes in their lives.*

These don't have to be climbing-Everest-level extremes. While small-talking, did your guest tell you they work as a cement layer? Try asking them about the *most dangerous thing* that ever happened on the job. Or about *the silliest* thing they've seen scrawled in wet cement. Or some variation on "What *most surprised* you when you started the job?"

Did your guest mention they have a super precocious kid? Ask about *the most surprising thing* the kid ever said. Is the kid a new driver? "What's the *most afraid you've ever been* as their passenger?"

Worst dates. Best dates. Most embarrassing thing ever. Proudest achievement ever. There tend to be interesting stories behind extreme moments, and everyone tends to have experienced a few. Your guests will tell you about them if you ask. And if for some reason they don't and then throw their Manhattan in your face, well, you'll have an extreme story of your own to tell.

RULE 3: THE TWO Ws

So now you've got your guest telling a story. But they may need your help to make it entertaining or illuminating. If you were a movie producer you would add sex, explosions, and Dwayne "The Rock" Johnson, but you're a dinner party host, so we suggest a different approach.

For decades, a wonderful Canadian Broadcasting Corporation vet named David Candow[6] was paid good money to make the rounds of public radio shows, teaching us all—among many other things—how to pull revealing tales out of interviewees. And a cornerstone of David's interviewing philosophy was *The Two Ws.*

It boils down to this: You know the six essential questions of journalism? Who, what, when, where, why, and how? To ensure that a guest's story becomes truly interesting, just ask two of those questions over and over: WHAT and WHY.

WHAT exactly happened? Seek specifics. Ideally just enough to entertainingly paint a picture, set a scene, and convey emotion. If a guest gets stuck on unimportant details, you ask, WHAT happened *next?* And WHAT did that feel like?

And then, most important of all: WHY was this event important?

This is where the guest's most thoughtful and emotional connection to a story lies. WHY did they behave the way they did? WHY does this event stand out in this person's head? WHY does it matter to them? WHY does it motivate them, or make them laugh or cry?[7]

What's amazing about "why" questions is that often the person telling the story doesn't even know the answers until you ask them. They may be surprised themselves at what they come up with. Or, even better, they may wonder what *you* think is important about their tale. Indeed, the funny thing about asking questions is that you know you're doing it right when your guest starts asking you questions back.[8] Guess what? That means NOW YOU ARE HAVING A CONVERSATION.

---

6   RIP David, 1940–2014.

7   Next time you listen to one of the great public radio storytelling shows, like *This American Life,* keep an ear out for some variation on the phrase "And that's when I realized…" What follows is the "Why" part of the story. It's *always* there.

8   Unless their question is something along the lines of "WHY ARE YOU BADGERING ME???" Then you're doing it wrong.

RULE 4: ASK QUESTIONS, NOT "GUESSES"

Another Candow tip. The point of asking questions is to get a guest to reveal something fascinating about themselves. And a quick way to *prevent* that from happening is to give them possible answers to your own question.

You'd be surprised how much this happens, both in real life and on radio shows, including our own. It's incredibly hard to avoid. And it goes something like this:

> HOST: Why was this story about how your mom knits
> beer koozies important to you? *Did it make you*
> *realize she loved you?*

The first question is fine. The problem with the second, italicized question is twofold. First of all, the guest might—and probably does—have a better, more unique and personal answer to your first question than the one you've provided. But often they'll feel obligated to at least consider *your* possible answer, rather than provide their own. And voilà, you've short-circuited what could've been a funny or surprising revelation.

The second problem with this question is, if your guest is shy or recalcitrant, it gives them a handy way to *avoid* revealing anything interesting about themselves—because it can easily be answered with a single word: "yes" or "no."

So you want to ask questions that *demand* interesting, thoughtful answers. Which counterintuitively are often much shorter and simpler questions. In the above example, you just lop off the end:

> HOST: Why was this story important to you?

Candow described this process as "bland in, interesting out."[9] A short, bland question (again, often preceded by the words "what" or "why") is more likely to provoke the guest to reveal colorful details and anecdotes you

---

9   Also a good descriptor of our personalities at home versus at work.

wouldn't otherwise know are inside them. It also puts them in a position to tell you the parts of a story *they* like the most, instead of the one you *imagined*.

Of course, the guest might still give you a super bland answer to your bland question. Like, "I dunno." But at least then it's not your fault for asking a bad question. It's *their* fault for being lame.

RULE 5: YOU DON'T GET TO BE COOL

Many of us media types have trained our whole lives to seem cool. Nothing fazes us. We've heard it all. When we light up our Gauloises, the world goes slo-mo, turns black-and-white, and a Velvet Underground tune swells in the background.

As a host, try to forget all that.[10] Your job is to create an atmosphere where people want to open up and share things they're excited about with each other, and they're not going to do that if they feel like you're disaffected and unmoved by anything.

One of our audio mentors, Peter Clowney, once did a radio piece about the legendary photographer Robert Capa. According to Peter, when Capa was asked how to capture great images of folks, he replied, "Like people, and let them know it." Same goes for making good conversation. Demonstrate that your goal is not to impress, but to *be impressed*. Through your questions, let them know you think their work or their interests or their experiences, commonplace though they may seem, are worthy of exploration—because they likely are.

If that proves difficult—if conversation turns to a topic you truly do know a ton about and have become bored with—well, we figure it's polite for a host to at least *feign* interest for a while.[11] Practice saying "Wow!," "Huh!," and "Really!" until the subject changes. And if the subject refuses to change, skip to the end of this chapter (part three, "Avoiding Black Holes").

---

10   Except the Velvet Underground part. Play as much Velvet Underground at your party as possible. Except "Sister Ray." And "All Tomorrow's Parties"—too obvious.

11   Also good practice for relationships.

RULE 6: REMEMBER YOUR AUDIENCE

A dinner party is a group affair. Whether or not everyone's actually throwing their two cents' worth into a conversation, all involved should be invested in what's being discussed. Don't leave some guests nodding their heads, pretending they know what's going on when they're actually clueless, yearning for the moment when they can hightail it home to their Netflix-and-ice-cream cocoon.

This means that constant clarification is required. If a guest is mumbling, restate a phrase or two for people who couldn't hear what was said. (On our show, you'll hear us do this constantly if we're interviewing someone over a noisy phone line.) If a guest makes an inside joke that half the table won't get, go ahead and laugh...and then put it in context for everyone. Add last names to first names so everyone knows who's being referred to. Even, again, if it makes you look uncool.

> *EXAMPLE: Film and TV star Rashida Jones attends Brendan's dinner party.*
>
> RASHIDA JONES: And that's when my dad finally acknowledged that I wasn't going to be a musician.
>
> BRENDAN: Your dad—Quincy Jones.
>
> GUEST #1: Duh.
>
> RASHIDA JONES: Yes, Guest #1, my father is very well-known—but thank you, Brendan, for clarifying that for those who might not be aware. As a reward, I would now like to passionately make out with you.[12]

RULE 7: ARE YOU STILL SHUTTING UP?

We know: it's next to impossible to stay all the way shut up. Keep trying.

---

12 Actual results may vary.

RULE 8: BE A "LADYLIKE BROAD"

"I have a penchant for green underwear."

This is something Anjelica Huston, Oscar-winning star of screen and stage, said whilst being interviewed on our show. Rico's response: "Wow. I did *not* expect to learn that today." If you could hear blushing on the radio, that's what it would sound like.

Ms. Huston said lots of other things—about her hallowed father, John, one of the greatest filmmakers of all time; about her early days in the insane go-go fashion world of the seventies. But what we most vividly remember from that conversation is two things: that she totally wears green underwear, and how cool she was for having told us so.

And yet revealing (pun intended) such intimate secrets flies in the face of what the etiquette pros call "polite conversation." We know this because we've had our regular etiquette pros Lizzie Post and Daniel Post Senning straight-up tell us: Sex, religion, and politics are potentially dangerous conversational territories through which one should tread carefully.

Lizzie and Dan are our pals, which is why we're comfortable saying that in our opinion, a quick way to turn your party dull is to worry too much about dangerous conversational territory. For us, actually, the most memorable conversations are the product of guests and hosts who dare to provoke, titillate, argue, and otherwise dance right into that territory. Indeed, when done right, being provocative can counterintuitively set fellow partygoers *more* at ease. Because they know they're not entering the social equivalent of Sunday school, where a misplaced cuss word—or stating a strong political opinion—will result in a knuckle beating from Sister Mary.

The trick is to create a permissive atmosphere with civility and style. The late, great Broadway star Elaine Stritch put it best while answering etiquette questions on our show. "The goal," she said, "is to be a *ladylike broad.*" Half civilized charmer, half wisecracking bomb thrower. The kind of person who should be able, Elaine suggested, "to lean across a table with a martini and say, 'What the *hell* are you talking about?!'"

For a historical example of a "ladylike broad," take Dorothy Parker—who'd probably not only tell you the color of her underwear, but would blithely let you know whether or not she was wearing it at the moment. On our own show, we'd probably point to Dick Cavett[13]—who managed to crack a joke about Grace Kelly's sex life *and* disparaged a pope without coming off as a jerkweed.

So how does he—and how can you—pull it off? It's not easy, but try this.

> a) *Copping to your own flaws:* Pointing out your own foibles can give you some license to point out others'. This is why comedians usually begin their set with a string of jokes about their own receding hairline, expanding waistline, or sorry sex life. After that, they're allowed to say whatever they want about anything.[14]
>
> b) *Be willing to GO THERE:* Letting slip a spicy detail or two about yourself signals to others that it's okay for them to do the same. Perhaps mention, in passing, the summer you juggled a few boyfriends... and a girlfriend, who happened to be a juggler.[15]
>
> c) *Smile/laugh:* A comedic lilt and a twinkle in one's eye can soften an otherwise caustic observation—your own or someone else's.

---

13 "Ladylike broad" here is gender-neutral.

14 EXCEPTION: Shouting racist epithets, a.k.a. the Michael Richards Rule.

15 Stop short of further details: the ladylike broad is clever, not vulgar. Innuendo is your friend.

d) *Remain calm:* If you're on the receiving end of someone's wit, accept it with humor. In other words, to encourage folks to dish it out, demonstrate how they should take it: with a cool head.

e) *Know when to ice the conversation:* Eventually someone will cross a conversational line even your tipsy and garrulous crew doesn't want crossed. This will usually be audibly denoted by everyone simultaneously groaning "Whooooaa." This is a good time to swap out the offender's wine for water, get up to put a new LP on the turntable (see chapter three), and change the subject.

f) *Be Anjelica Huston, Elaine Stritch, Dorothy Parker, or Dick Cavett.*

❧ ❧ ❧

"Don't behave. Misbehave."

— PEACHES

❧ ❧ ❧

PART 2: TALKING POLITICS

When we solicit questions for our etiquette segment, some of the most common emails[16] we get are from listeners desperate to know how to engage in political conversations that won't result in a murder-suicide.

This gives us hope. Because if the world's increasing inability to get along is evidence of anything, it's that people with opposing views aren't talking to each other enough. Forget politeness—they're barely conversing at all.[17]

---

16 Actually, as previously noted, the most common emails we get come from foreign countries offering Viagra for just $9.99. But the political question is a close second.

17 Attacking each other on Twitter doesn't count. See strategy number two, this section.

And why would they be? In a polarized political world, there seems less and less reason to talk with the other side. It feels like an exercise in futility that can at best result in a screaming fight, and at worst in a climactic scene from a Quentin Tarantino film. Neither is an awesome dinner party scenario.

Problem is, we don't have any choice. It's like a highway: The only way for people to safely share the road is to use turn signals. To share a country, we have to hear each other out.[18][19] And if we can't talk in an atmosphere as warm and low-stakes as a dinner party, we're certainly not going to pull it off in the kiln of assholery that is national politics.

We don't have the perfect solution to engender bipartisan chitchat. If we did, at this moment our planet would be awash in way less fear and rage, and way more good vibes, understanding, calypso music, and pie-judging contests. But we've got a few strategies that might allow you to have a polit-ical conversation with your friend's husband Owen in a way that lets you walk away respecting each other. Or at least without cutting his ear off with the electric carving knife. And that's a good start.

#1

DON'T EXPECT MIRACLES

You're not going to convince a lifelong liberal, over Chablis and tikka mas-ala, that it's perfectly okay to own an arsenal of AR15s. The perfect retort will not instantly convince a conservative that we should all be taxed in order to fund performance art.

Think about the last time you truly changed your mind about some-thing important.[20] It probably happened over the course of years. Or after

---

18   And also use turn signals. It's the rod with the arrows on it sticking out of your steer-ing column.

19   By the way, and it's amazing we have to even mention this in the twenty-first century, but you *don't* have to hear out actual Nazis/white supremacists. Most of the planet fought a world war so we wouldn't have to tolerate hate speech at the table, thanks.

20   Having second thoughts about buying this book doesn't count. Anyway, you can't return it now; the spine is damaged from when you threw it across the room.

something crazily momentous happened, like a health scare, or your sibling suddenly being genuinely nice to you. It almost certainly *didn't* happen over one discussion at a party.

This is especially true of political beliefs. According to a study by economists Ethan Kaplan and Sharun Mukand, political affiliations are one of the hardest habits to break. Once you declare yourself a member of a political party—often as a teenager—you end up on that party's mailing lists and get exposed to a steady diet of their agenda/propaganda, and thus a certain set of beliefs gets reinforced over and over again. For decades.

So, our advice? Accept this. It's amazing how much chiller a political argument becomes when you understand you don't have to, and in fact won't, "win" it tonight. State your best case, and when you find yourself *re*stating it over and over, declare a truce and move on to talking about the new *Star Wars*.[21]

#2
ATTACK A POLICY, NOT A PERSON

True or false: A great way to get someone to take your ideas seriously is to call them an idiot fascist racist backward uneducated dumbass redneck hypocrite who votes against their own best interests because they are a mindless sheep.[22]

False, right? The correct answer is "false," guys.

And yet this is a tactic that folks of all political persuasions resort to an awful lot. Don't do it. It will not change someone's mind. It will reinforce their belief that folks who disagree with them are mean and bad. And they will have a point.

By the way, the same goes for personally insulting politicians with whom your rival politically aligns. That tactic can backfire, actually gener-

---

21   For better or worse, there will, from now on, always be a new *Star Wars*.

22   Or, conversely, say that they are a condescending terrorist-hugging libtard snowflake Communist whiner who never did an honest day's work for a living and hates America.

ating *sympathy*[23] for the corrupt despotic cretin you believe should be removed from office and indicted on federal charges of being an idiot.

Instead, take a cue from Gandhi. Not his fashion sense—few among us are cool enough to pull off attending a dinner party wearing a homemade sheet—but his political tactics. Gandhi's most galvanizing protest action wasn't directed against any specific British politician. It was a protest against the Brits' draconian salt tax.

In other words, dispute the value of a political policy. Not the value of the human being who supports it.

#3
DETAILS, PLEASE

Of course, even if *you* avoid personal attacks, you can't always count on your guests to exercise similar restraint. Luckily, acclaimed author George Saunders—who according to the MacArthur Foundation is a genius—once told us about his favorite tactic for maintaining civility: asking for specifics.

In writing workshops, he said, "someone will say something kind of hurtful, and the only way out of that is to keep asking the person to be more and more specific. So, you know, 'Your story sucks, I hate it!' can get talked down to 'Page four lags a bit in energy.' And the latter is very easy to hear."

The same device can be deployed in political conversations:

"The mayor is a bum!" shouts your overexcited guest.

"What specifically did he do?" you ask calmly.

"He increased parking fines!"

---

23   Example: Being the butt of constant personal derision arguably helped Italian right-winger Silvio Berlusconi *consolidate* power. According to University of Chicago professor Luigi Zingales, the effect of the attacks "was to increase Mr. Berlusconi's popularity. His secret was an ability to set off a Pavlovian reaction among his leftist opponents, which engendered instantaneous sympathy in most moderate voters."

Poof! Now you're talking about parking fines. You are discussing a policy, not a person. Your guest should thank you for making the conversation way less likely to result in a screaming match. But don't count on it.

#4

MAKE THIS ALL ABOUT YOU

Bummer news for those who embrace Enlightenment principles: A growing body of psychological data indicates that trying to reason with people using logic, truth, and facts might be fruitless.[24] Getting someone to change a fiercely held belief can be like trying to convince a cat to drop a dead mouse from its jaws: They will cling to it *even more intensely*.

Luckily, there's more data that indicates there may be an antidote: empathy.[25] If you can get someone to empathize with you—showing how a political issue affects you *personally*—you can potentially alter their outlook, or at least get them to hear you out. Comedian Cristela Alonzo put it to us like this: "There is no point in name-calling people that don't agree with you. *But it's actually hard for them to negate your experience of what you've lived*" [italics ours].

That means: Try leading with a *personal* story, instead of data or statistics. It's easy for someone to say the government should get out of the health insurance business. But it's hard for them to disregard your story about the time you couldn't afford insurance, got an infected finger from a hangnail, and the trip to the emergency room nearly bankrupted your family. (Although be prepared for them to tell you to just stop picking your nails, dude.)

---

24 For examples thereof, see the 2010 *Boston Globe* article tellingly titled "How Facts Backfire."
25 Wrote Lisa Miller in a 2016 *New York* magazine article, "Even a little compassionate contact with what social scientists call 'out group' members—that is, people who aren't like you—can have an enduring impact."

KEEP MIXING IT UP

If you ask us, the most important thing is to continue doing what you're doing: seeking out new conversations. Keep hosting and attending gatherings where one or two of the guests are people you don't 1,000 percent agree with. *Even if politics isn't discussed,* you have shown by example that those of your political persuasion do not hate or fear those of opposing views. Eventually, if talk *does* turn to politics, they'll be a lot more likely to listen.

And in the long term, we firmly believe this sort of thing *can* lead to real change. Barney Frank, the first congressman to voluntarily come out of the closet, told us that when he entered Congress in the early eighties, working in government was considered noble, but being openly gay was verboten. When he retired a few decades later? Working in government was frowned upon, but being openly gay was acceptable. He said that by the time he married his male partner, his Republican colleagues' biggest problem with it was that many of them weren't invited to the wedding.

If that can happen in Congress, it can happen over a series of nice dinners.

❧ ❧ ❧

"We have hierarchies of all different kinds in this country, and I find that [...] if you just listen, *you discover that those hierarchies don't mean too much. That your expectations are almost always wrong."*
— GLORIA STEINEM

❧ ❧ ❧

PART 3: AVOIDING BLACK HOLES

Despite your best efforts, certain guests can dominate a conversation, draining all the fun and energy from it, like a black hole consuming a nearby star.[26] Here are a few examples, along with strategies for shepherding the party through these dark times.

THE AGGRESSIVE BORE

The guest who has A LOT to say, about nothing. Stories which merit a single sentence, like "I wanted to return a razor to Walgreens, but I lost the receipt," become Greek epics. Each detail of purchasing the razor, its eventual malfunction, and the search for the receipt are recounted, loudly and dramatically. And yet the story *has no drama*. There is no surprise twist, no insightful resolution to the Aggressive Bore's tales. There is only misplaced passion and volume.

This guest is usually also friendly and gregarious, so people feel bad about wanting to shut them up. On their behalf, *you must try*.

Containment Strategy: Lie/Interrupt/Deflect

The moment an Aggressive Bore launches into an anecdote,

a) FEIGN INTEREST in it for a few seconds.

b) DISINGENUOUSLY INTERRUPT by uttering the magic phrase "I don't mean to interrupt." Then explain that the Bore just said something that reminds you of a story *another* guest recently told you.

c) DEFLECT: Point to said guest and insist they tell that story, *immediately*. Choose a guest you know has a rich backlog of anecdotes. Note: The story you encourage them to tell needn't have anything to do with the story the Bore was telling.

---

26   For an especially cool example of this occurring, Google "Swift J1644+57." But not at the dinner table, for risk of encouraging others to fish out their own smartphones, ironically creating a conversational black hole.

EXAMPLE:

BORE
Oh my God, the other day I ate some yogurt!

YOU
(feigning interest)
Hmm!

BORE
It was *crazy!* First off, I went to the drugstore, the
one down the street next to the taco truck. And then —

YOU
(disingenuously interrupting)
Oooh, **I don't mean to interrupt!** But Jayden, you were telling me
an amazing story earlier about taco trucks, weren't you?

JAYDEN
No, I was telling you about a pregnant woman I met who
was walking the Pacific Crest Trail.

YOU
Oh right, right. Tell everyone about it!

*Note: After Jayden has told this interesting tale, the Aggressive Bore will attempt
to tell their boring tale again. Just repeat the above steps as necessary.*

THE MUSIC SNOB

The Music Snob is not to be confused with your standard-issue Hipster Music
Geek. The Music Snob has entered a whole different, deeply jaded geek realm.

The Snob collects music and music trivia not so he[27] can share it with others, but because he doesn't have much else going on in his sad life. He seeks the most esoteric music possible because it is the only thing that makes him unique. The Music Snob isn't a big fan of the Rolling Stones...but he's really been digging the Ronnie Wood "Guitar-Restringing Tapes" bootleg from Nepal.

No one else at the party has heard the music the Music Snob talks incessantly about. They're not having fun listening to the Music Snob talk about it. Hell, *he's* not having fun either—the only reason the dude's still talking is because if he stops, the conversation might turn to another subject, and he *knows* no other subject. Pity the poor Music Snob. Pity him, and then put a stop to him.

Containment Strategy: The "Track Five" Pivot

a) Proudly DECLARE your latest musical obsession: the fifth song off a favorite album of your childhood, ideally by a popular but not critically celebrated act. For Brendan that would be George Michael's "Cowboys and Angels." For Rico it's "Carmella" by Taco.

Neither song is actually that great. Indeed, Track Fives are generally unmemorable. Perfect—even if the Snob's heard it, he won't remember a thing about it.

b) ASSURE the Snob that this track is an underappreciated find of immense musical importance.

c) ACKNOWLEDGE that this seems impossible. But say the British music magazine *Mojo* recently did a whole article about it.

d) Now *quickly* PIVOT and open the conversation to the other guests: What childhood music have *they* revisited lately?

---

27 We're not going to bother using gender-neutral pronouns in this section: the Music Snob is *always* male.

YOU
(declaring)
You know what I've been getting back into?
Great White's "Mista Bone." Off their album
Twice Shy?

SNOB
(confused)
"Mista Bone"?

YOU
Yes. I **assure** you that it bridged the gap between
eighties baroque New Wave and nineties downtown
squonkcore jazz.

SNOB
(in disbelief)
Seriously? Great White?

YOU
Yes. *Mojo* magazine *just did a whole article about it.*
(**pivoting** to other guests)
What'd *you* guys listen to growing up?

DEEPLY UNHIP GUEST
Oh, I've never stopped loving Richard Marx!

Poof! You have now successfully turned the Snob's monologue about *obscure* music into a group conversation about *mediocre* music. Hey, small victories.

We're all for talking about money around the dinner table. That old taboo forbidding us from discussing each other's salaries? We suspect that's just a conspiracy by The Man to keep us in the dark about fair wages, and to protect our friend Stacey who always claims she's too broke to buy us a round.

But Business Dude doesn't have equality on his mind. He's just obsessed with deal making and cash. And especially with how much of the latter you used to obtain various items in your home.

"You paid a ton for the roast, amiright?" bellows Business Dude from across the kitchen.

"Great wine!" he exclaims at the dinner table. "Tastes like a forty-buck Chuck to me!"

"Hahaha!" you hear him chuckling from the garage, which you thought you locked but he's somehow found a way into. "I bet my watch is more expensive than your Subaru!"

Business Dude can turn a night of leisure into an episode of *The Price Is Right*—*Sadist Edition*. Neutralize him.

Containment Strategy: Send Out the Clown

a) Praise Business Dude's acumen. Clearly, he knows quality and value when he sees it! Tell him that is why...

b) You want to enlist him to go buy something you suddenly desperately need for the party. Or, to use language he'll understand, you want to EMPOWER him to LEVERAGE HIS CORE COMPETENCIES by TASKING him with a wine run.

c) Promise you'll pay him back later. This will earn you his respect—since *he* knows that *you* know a proper guest would never ask a host to pay him back for a bottle of wine.

Note: This will separate Business Dude from the party for only the duration of his wine run. Thus, for best results, tell him that the most exclusive and expensive liquor store in town is ten miles away down a busy freeway.

THE OUTRAGED POLITICAL JUNKIE

As outlined above, we're big fans of political conversation at the dinner table. But Outraged Political Junkies (OPJs) are not fans of conversation. They're fans of being *outraged*. About *everything*. And *blaming people* for it. At length.

The OPJ is often an elderly person who spends way too much time watching a politically polarized cable news channel. By the time they arrive at your party, they want nothing more than to express their frustration at the evils they've been told are all around them.

The problem is, even if everyone at the table shares this guest's political views, they probably aren't eager to hear a thirty-minute rant about them. After a while, the OPJ is just someone screaming about really depressing things while everyone's trying to enjoy some coffee cake. Make it stop.

Containment Strategy: The WWII Defense

Many OPJs lived through — or had parents who lived through — World War II. Gently remind them that during that war, thirty countries engaged in six years of "total warfare" during which upwards of fifty million people were killed, including the systematic genocide of six million Jews and the flattening of two Japanese cities with atomic bombs.

Things are bad these days, respected elder, but they ain't *that* bad.[28]

---

28 Admittedly *yet*.

Alternative Strategy: The Digital Surrender

If that doesn't work, break out the smartphone and divert everyone's attention with the cutest cat video you can find. We know, we know. But desperate times demand desperate measures.

OTHER POSSIBLE CONVERSATION
DERAILERS

Alas, we have a maximum word count for this book, and we've still got a chapter to go. So good luck dealing with these guys.

The Constant-Life-Crisis Person
The "Have You Seen?"er
The Spoiler Alarmist
The Me Me Me
The Cologne Bather
The Extreme Beatles Hater
Fuckin' Todd

CHAPTER SEVEN

THE AFTERMATH

If your dinner party was a video game, at this point in the evening, peppy eight-bit jams would blare from your stereo as the following words hovered, shimmering, above your head:

!!!Dinner Party Magic Zone!!!

Congratulations—you've done it! Take a good look around. Bellies are full. Spirits are high. Everyone you see now owes *you* dinner. So what if the hake recipe called for marjoram but you used mayonnaise? That's all behind you now. See that dewy glow on everyone's face? That's the dewy glow of satisfaction. Or possibly the dewy glow of having just pounded down a ton of food and booze in a home that's super hot from your oven. Either way, people are happy. They either want to bed you or *be* you. Cats, for a brief moment, consider the possibility that being human might be more awesome than being a cat, and then lick their bellies and fall back asleep.

That feeling you feel—that feeling is joy. It's what Aristotle felt when he learned that Plato didn't copyright his ideas. It's how Einstein felt when he realized he didn't have to comb his hair anymore. You have reached dinner party nirvana.

Enjoy it. This feeling will last anywhere between fifteen seconds and fifteen minutes. Then it's back to business.

PART 1: THE THREE PATHS

Now that dinner is over, it's time to work on the most "party" part of the dinner party. We at D.E.C.E.N.T. (Dinner Party Executive Council Ensuring Nifty Times), during our seminal October 2005 conference at Todd's Bar and Grill in Playa Del Rey, identified three distinct paths down which you can now lead your guests. Choose one and get cracking.

PATH 1: THE CLASSIC (A.K.A. CHILLING)

The most common end to a weekday dinner party, "Chilling" is also the post-dinner-party style preferred by chatty people, lazy people, and those who like to keep nibbling and sipping, even though they just had a full meal and a bunch of booze.

For best Chilling results, transition from the dining table to the living room. If a living room is not available, either a) transition careers so you can afford one, or simply b) clear the table and hang out there some more.

The point of Chilling is to wind down any serious conversation or antic high jinks, and conclude the evening with a calm period of warmth and mellowness. It's a time for mutual reflection over cognac and roasted chestnuts (or, more likely, chips 'n' wine dregs), with long pauses for contented sighs. A time to share belly-laugh-inducing personal stories. Or a time to not talk at all: some may choose to doze off, or stare at the popcorn ceiling and imagine it is the surface of the Moon. All that's required is at least two people engaging in conversation, plus groovy background music, preferably with lots of reverb.

If there's a marijuana smoker at your party—now's *definitely* her time to shine. Assuming yours is a THC-tolerant crowd, let that sister get everyone baked. Otherwise, invite her to step outside, where she can pot-vape alone and wonder what happened to that little girl who wanted to be a ballerina.

Chilling's a pretty casual affair. Showing each other photos on your phone is even permitted (though only as brief exhibits to enhance conversation). One caveat: If things get so casual someone unbuckles the top button of their pants, hurricane belches, and starts murmuring "Tummy happy, nap, nap," you're Chilling too hard and it's probably time for the party to end.

PATH 2: THE PDPDP (POST-DINNER-PARTY DANCE PARTY)

Dancing is like vertically having sex with one or several people, in public, while fully clothed. You should do it as much as possible.

Sadly, as we get older, opportunities to dance dwindle. We grow more afraid of looking silly, and also our cartilage turns to dry cork. This is precisely why the tail end of a dinner party is the perfect time to dance: Everyone is now friends, everyone is loose, and Band-Aids and compression wraps are in your medicine cabinet nearby.

The trick with the PDPDP is you can't force it. Do not leap up, flick the lights on and off, shout "DANCE PARTYYYY," and begin gyrating alone in the center of the room. This will frighten your guests. They will also suspect—possibly correctly—that you just took a snort of pep powder without inviting them.

Instead, await the slightly up-tempo disco track you cleverly dropped into your party playlist to facilitate *exactly this moment* (see chapter three, part two, "Preparing the Music"). Nod your head or tap your foot along to the rhythm. Perhaps take a fellow guest's hand and, still seated, begin ironically-except-kind-of-sincerely swaying it back and forth in a vaguely dance-like way. *Then* rise with them and set the dance party in motion. Others will soon take your cue.[1]

Wait ten minutes or so after dancing begins before introducing that big phat booty-bouncing sex jam that really raises the roof. Otherwise you might scare off shyer participants before their inhibitions are shed. WARNING: This is the part of the night when frisky people, particularly the drunkest ones, forget about the "fully clothed" part of dancing. Monitor misbehavior, and be prepared to dance the mashed potato between people you know would be a disaster together.

This is also the part of the party during which you are most likely to hear a loud knocking at the door. That is your neighbor, ready to kill you. Oh, did we forget to tell you to tell them in advance that you might be having a late-night dance party tonight? Yes: we did that so you'd have plausible deniability when you now say to them that you had *no idea* the noise would be so bothersome. Apologize, turn down the music, and relish feeling like a salty teenage punk.

PATH 3: ADULT ACTIVITIES

We're not talking about orgies and paying bills. Though if you can make the former happen, hey—achievement unlocked, you. No, we're talking about parlor games,[2] sing-alongs, and their ilk.

This path is most common at Friday night Gen X dinner parties, when no one wants to end the festivities early, but everyone's tired from having worked all day. Adult activities provide a little spark of mild competition to

---

1   Or they'll completely bail into the kitchen so they can continue their conversation without you and your dance partner's butt wiggling in their faces. Should this occur, give up, slowly turn down the music, and revert to path one.

2   Way back in chapter one, we noted that game nights are not dinner parties, as they give the party a purpose beyond dining and partying. But at this point, you're deploying games to *extend* the partying; they're just a spice to zing up the main dish, which has been lying out too long and is threatening to spoil.

make up for the raw adrenaline that used to power you into the wee hours back in college and which you now lack. If a dinner party is recess for adults, think of this as the dodgeball portion of the evening.

Parlor Games

We suggest sticking to the classics—but not *too* classic (see "Parlor Games of Yore," below). For example:

CHARADES: Recommended if one or several of your guests are cooler/more famous than everyone else. Charades levels the playing field by making *everybody* look foolish. Also, like other old-school activities such as drinking Scotch and living in New York City, people will say they enjoyed it even if they didn't.

CELEBRITY: A kind of modern update on charades, wherein the names of celebrities are scribbled onto scraps of paper that are then folded and placed in a bowl. Teams of two then see how many of the names they can guess in a minute, based on abbreviated clues. Becomes really fun when a snob who just got his MFA puts only the names of obscure Russian playwrights in the bowl, making everyone else mad.

EXQUISITE CORPSE: In this game, a sheet of paper is folded into sections. Each guest draws part of a body on a section, without looking at the other sections, to create a weird mutant beast. Exquisite corpse was invented by the early surrealists—thus the MFA snob guy will probably recommend playing it.

THAT GAME FROM *INGLOURIOUS BASTERDS* WHERE PEOPLE PUT CARDS ON THEIR FOREHEADS, a.k.a. "Who Am I?": That's a good one. Make sure all pistols and shotguns are removed from the room beforehand.

Card/Board Games

Card games kind of frighten us because they rely on two of our least favorite parts of high school: math and cutthroat competition. And yet we see the pleasure in breaking out a deck and engaging in an old-world pastime with friends. To keep things friendly, we suggest non-gambling card games. That means gin, rummy, pinochle, canasta…really any game with a name that sounds like a cocktail. Therefore Uno is also acceptable, while seven-card Texas Hold'em is not.

If you want to avoid numbers altogether, stick to interactive "social" card games like Cards Against Humanity (if no family members are present) or Apples to Apples (if they are), which are more about facilitating conversation than crushing your competition.

Also acceptable: traditional board games which can be completed in a relatively short period of time, like Sorry!

DO NOT PLAY MONOPOLY. It will last for two hours and by the end someone will hate someone.

LIKEWISE, SCRABBLE, because of the one person who takes fifteen minutes to finally put down "CAT" for five points. And don't even get us started about RISK.

☀ PARLOR GAMES OF YORE ☀

From the Victorian era, we've inherited many games—charades among them—which delight partygoers even today. Other entertainments of the gas lamp period, however, did not withstand the test of time. A partial list:

Lint Picking
Shuttlecock Repair

Mock-the-Urchin

What's That Noise?

Damn Fine Smoking Pipe!

Yell at Maude

Atlas Perusal

Avoiding Polio

Brass Compass Polishing

Breathing Whilst Corseted

Not Making Out at All with Anyone

Sing-Alongs

Gathering around an acoustic guitar isn't just for hippies anymore. In fact, over the past few years, musical practice spaces have become the hunting lodges of a certain brand of urban American male—the place they go to get away from their families, drink beer, smoke cigarettes, and push buttons and levers on expensive pieces of technology. Except instead of bringing home meat and a fear of government overreach, they bring home songs.

The end of a dinner party is a perfect outlet to try out one or two of those[3]...and then to get over yourself and launch into cover tunes everyone knows. This is supposed to be a time for communal interactivity, not a showcase for your nascent indie rock career. Also: NO MORE THAN TWO SONGS PER SINGER. Otherwise you are not having a dinner party, you are having a nightclub with a headliner.

---

3   Poetry readings are also a good fit for this post-dinner path. But the poems must make sense to the average person. So in practice this never happens.

* ⋏ ⋎

*"The number of times I get asked to sing 'Willkommen'…
Seriously, it must be thousands of times. People
think, 'Wouldn't it be fun if you sang "Willkommen"?!'
I'm like, 'No.'"*

— Cabaret star Alan Cumming, on the cover
you shouldn't ask him to sing

* ⋏ ⋎

PART 2: CLEANUP

The finish line approacheth! You've now chilled for an hour or two. Or your stupid old legs just can't dance any longer. Or you've all realized one of the guests is a ringer at canasta and there's no point in trying to beat her. The party is winding down. At this point in the evening, you will realize your household is in one of two states of cleanliness.

The first and most desirable is a kind of cozy, ramshackle disorder. Guests have thumbed through your books and scattered them across the dining room table. Record albums are piled in front of the stereo. A tower of plates and silverware, topped with a crown of chicken bones, rises precariously from your kitchen sink, and on every flat surface sits an emptied wineglass. It's the kind of mess that makes a home feel lived-in. You gaze upon it with a sense of quiet satisfaction at a job well done.

The second state of cleanliness might best be described as "Dresden, Germany, February 1945." Total wreckage. Holes have been knocked through your drywall. Broken shards of glass and porcelain crunch underfoot. Your favorite chair somehow has only three legs now; a drunk guest tries to sit in it and crashes ass-first to the floor. Your tablecloth is shiny with a crust of melted candle wax and spilled sauces. Soiled dishes lie anywhere but in the sink.

There's one in the cat box. Why?! There is no reason. Piled in a corner of your kitchen are five overstuffed garbage bags, torn and leaking a fragrant slurry of shrimp tails, olive pits, tomato guts, and beer onto the linoleum. Already flies are swarming in anticipation of the mighty feast that awaits them. You can practically hear their tiny fly tongues, licking their hairy little lips.

It's the kind of mess that crushes the soul. You gaze upon it and pray for blindness.

If you find yourself in this second scenario, the first thing to do is take a breath and understand that it's late, you are very tired, you've probably ingested a lot of salt, and you're beginning to be hungover. Your perspective is a little warped—really, *this mess is not as bad as it seems.*

Second of all, we're going to get you through it step by step. Starting with a cry for help.

CRYING FOR HELP

Here's the bad news: Though a polite guest will offer to help clean up, the polite host's duty is to refuse the offer.[4]

Firstly, because neither guests nor YOU should be spending these last few precious minutes of social time trying to get gravy stains out of the rug. Relish this time! Reality can wait!

And secondly, your guests are as tired as you are, but they're not lucky enough to be standing ten feet away from their bed. They have a walk/drive/cab ride/subway trip yet to deal with. What's more, to attend your party, some of these people are dropping sixty bucks an hour on babysitters. They're not spending that cash for the privilege of scraping dried Parm out of your pasta bowls. Don't make them.

---

4   If they insist on helping anyway, wonderful. But assume they won't. Most guests proffer help *knowing* you're supposed to refuse it, thereby freeing them to pound down more cheese cubes before hitting the road. No worries: This means you're allowed to pull the same move when they invite you to *their* dinner party.

There are, however, a scant handful of circumstances where it's okay to conscript/trick your guests into cleaning up.

Clearing the Table

Most guests understand it's their duty to help clear the dinner table. Let them. Moving plates from the table to the sink is easy and makes people feel like they contributed, without getting their hands dirty. It creates table space around which Chilling or Parlor Games can occur. Most importantly, it ensures that dirty plates are hidden in the kitchen as swiftly as possible, so you can pretend they don't exist until later.

Garbage Hauling (a.k.a. the Waif Rule)

You have a giant garbage bag full of stinking wine and whiskey bottles. It weighs two tons and must be moved outside to the recycling bin before the cockroach armies come to slurp. The problem is, you are a waif with all the upper body strength of a tiny baby. Or perhaps you were recently injured, or are disabled. Or maybe your home is in the kind of neighborhood where one can be mugged three times between your back door and the recycling bin. In all these circumstances, it's okay to sweetly ask the biggest, muscliest guest[5] at your party to take out the garbage for you. Go ahead: it'll make them feel like a hero.

The Dishwashing Bestie

Back in chapter five, we exhorted you to seat your best pal next to you at dinner. But maybe you couldn't. Maybe you had to displace them with a lech (see chapter five, part two, "The Throw-Yourself-on-the-Grenade

---

5   This person can also be enlisted to help you move furniture before and after the party if necessary, or to pry open jelly jars. Just constantly praise their strength and ask where they work out—they love that.

Exception"). If so, a cunning way to squeeze in some one-on-one time with your bestie is by whisking them away to the kitchen to help you out with the dishes...provided you keep two things in mind.

1) YOU CLEAN, THEY DRY. You've brought them in here mainly to dish, not to *do* dishes. A good host does not force a guest to plunge their hands into greasy sink water with little pieces of lettuce floating around in it.

2) THIS MAY END YOUR PARTY. Launching the dishwashing process is a universal signal that the party is ending, and that you want guests to leave. So either make it clear that you want the party to continue in your absence, or be prepared to emerge from the kitchen with your pal to find a scene straight out of *28 Days Later*, your home eerily emptied of humanity, as if they were never there.

Food Pawning

A good party ends with two things: a warm feeling in your soul, and between ten and a hundred pounds of leftovers. Some of these you'll consume during whatever cleanup you punt to tomorrow. The rest you'll have to store (or not; see sidebar "Leftovers: What to Keep and What to Burn").

But packing all that stuff away takes time. It also means you're creating future dishes for yourself, in the form of soiled storage containers which will eventually have to be cleaned when you finish eating the leftovers. *If* you eat them. In many cases, they will take up space for weeks, getting pushed further and further to the back of the fridge, until finally you rediscover them, with a whole little mold civilization growing on top, and chuck them in the compost bin.

Solution? Make your *guests* take some leftovers home. No, please, you insist! If it means letting them also take home your baking dish, in which sit the last two servings of paella, fine: that's a baking dish you don't have to clean.[6] In fact, they'll probably clean it *for* you, before returning it. A year from now.

> *"If you brought a dish [to my party], take it with you,*
> *because I'm going to take it to Goodwill in one week.*
> *Because that's on you. That's on you."*
> — BETH DITTO

◂ ◂ ◂

Your Good Morning Maid

Perhaps you let a drunk guest crash on your couch overnight. When they awaken the next morning, you are officially no longer having a dinner party (see chapter one, part one, "Time"). Therefore, dinner party rules no longer apply, and you're free to consider this guest your personal janitorial staff for the ensuing two hours. Have them scour the toilet, wash windows, paint your walls, or build that backyard fence you've been meaning to erect. In return, they get coffee. And leftovers.

WHAT YOU NEED TO CLEAN TONIGHT

After exploiting guests as much as possible using the above selfish justifications, you will now be faced with a bunch of stuff to clean on your own. What can wait till morning?

Frankly, *all* of it. You've done quite enough for one day, thank you, and you deserve blessed rest. Just understand that you're only going to become

---

6   WARNING: Some guests will attempt the reverse maneuver, by "accidentally" leaving behind food and dishes they brought to the party, which they don't want to transport home or clean. Be vigilant! As they leave, present them with a grocery bag full of all their things. Perhaps with some stuff you want to get rid of hidden in there as well.

more hungover as time passes—cleanup isn't going to be easier tomorrow. Also, you will likely awaken to questionable scents. And possibly a bunch of tiny new insect friends. Therefore, a checklist of the stuff you might want to deal with before the sun rises on the wreckage.

1. Things That Can Hurt You

Broken glass, skewers and knives lying on the floor, copies of books written by hate-filled talk radio personalities strategically left behind by your one friend's spouse...you don't want to stumble upon any of that tomorrow morning. Sweep your place clean of them now.

2. Fish

We told you. We *told* you not to cook fish. But you did, and now you must face the consequences. You should have refrigerated any uneaten fish within two hours of serving it. If you didn't, trash it before someone eats it and gets sick. Then super fast get the garbage bag with the fish in it into a dumpster outside. Hurry the hell up: it isn't getting any less smelly.

3. Things Ants Want

A.k.a. all food. If you live in an area with ants, you are going to have to make sure *no* food from the party remains anywhere the ants can get to. Meaning everywhere. Don't delay. The ants come quickly. They are organized and relentless. They're probably watching you reading this book right now. Waiting.

4. Things Pets Will Destroy or Sicken Themselves With

During the party, you or your guests could oversee your pets. Or maybe you shut them away in another room where they couldn't get into trouble. But as you sleep, they will once again have free rein. Records and record sleeves left unprotected on the floor become fun chew toys or scratching pads. Half-empty wineglasses will become *fully* empty as your pets knock them

BRUNCH IS HELL

203

THE AFTERMATH

onto the white rug. They will find the deadly fish you didn't trash and eat it. We told you not to cook fish. We *told* you.

5. Stains

Some food stains must be treated immediately, or they set forever. Interestingly, most methods of removing food stains involve deploying *other* foods. Did you know you can use beer to remove tea or coffee stains? Also, salt and white vinegar works on light carpet stains. Of course, after you deploy these methods, your stain-free home will smell like a British pub after an upset win in the World Cup. Your call.

To be honest, most stains probably happened earlier in the evening, and if you've waited till now to deal with them it's too late anyway; go to sleep. And if you live in student housing, don't bother. Tomorrow your roommate is just going to spill bong water in the same spot.

6. Dishes

Ignore most of these for now. But soak pots with egg, rice, or strands of pasta grafted onto them overnight — or you'll need a pickax to get it off tomorrow. Also, clean a few utensils and dishes. That way you can use them in the morning to eat leftovers, which you'll need to fortify yourself for cleaning everything else.

Note: If your spouse/domestic partner is hosting a dinner party, YOU are ALSO hosting the dinner party. Even if you didn't want to have the dinner party at all, and argued like hell against it. Everything expected of your now *co*host is also expected of you. Grin and bear it.

You are also expected to help clean up afterward — *even if your spouse/ domestic partner assured you in advance that you wouldn't have to.*[7] That is

---

7   Exception: If you want your relationship to end.

something spouses/domestic partners say. They might even mean it. That doesn't mean they won't silently resent you for sitting there watching *The Shawshank Redemption* again while they ant-proof the kitchen at 1 a.m.

LEFTOVERS: WHAT TO KEEP AND WHAT TO BURN

You've pawned off all the food you want to/are able to. Now you've got to decide what to do with the rest. Store it or toss it? If you cook regularly, go ahead and save almost all of it. For the rest of you, here's a list of what you can pack into the composter instead.

DRESSED SALAD

By morning it will be a green mush with cherry tomatoes on top.

FRIED POTATOES

They will congeal into a cold, chewy loaf of gray.

RICE

Put it in the fridge, and a few hours later, congratulations! You have created a brick made of tiny pieces of white gravel. You can reenergize the rice brick by using it for fried rice the next day. But really consider whether you're gonna make fried rice the next day.

BAGUETTE

Use it tonight to sop up the delicious grease at the bottom of your roasting pan, because by tomorrow what you will have is a tooth-shatteringly hard, baguette-shaped crouton. This can actually be used in a variety of dishes, but you aren't going to cook those.

CHICKEN BONES

They are the essential ingredient in homemade soup. Are you going to make homemade soup? No? Trash.

> ### RENDERED BACON FAT
>
> Earlier today, to make room for ice in your freezer, you threw away the previous tub of this you saved. Now you're going to try saving some again? You aren't a colonial pioneer; you're never going to use this.
>
> P.S.: Yes, we know, trashing food is decadent and wasteful. Solutions: 1) Learn to cook with leftovers. 2) Make everyone at the party eat more. Or 3) provide them with less food, upending centuries of cultural conditioning that says hosts should present guests with abundance. Good luck with that last one.

PART 3: GOODBYES

"When can I say goodbye?"

It sounds like the title of a Morrissey song, but it's actually what you're thinking right about now. When, you wonder, is it okay to indicate to your guests that it's time to hit the road and leave you to sober up and begin cleaning?

You may not have to. Departure proceedings often begin naturally, like a tornado. A guest peeks at their phone, someone yawns, and suddenly the magic protective bubble surrounding your dinner party is swept away, as the grim realization sets in that the real world cannot be avoided. The real world: where bosses, children, and debtors roam; where food is not free; and where sobriety is expected.

But if that doesn't happen, at a certain point it's perfectly within your rights as host to say—sweetly, always sweetly—"Hey, I think I gotta kick you guys out." The question remains, though: When? Provide yourself with an answer by tracing a path through the following chart.

SHOULD I KICK THESE GUYS OUT?

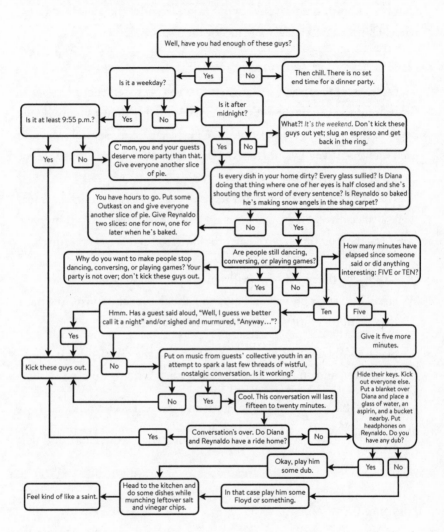

Can you almost taste it? You're about to successfully end a perfect dinner party! Holy shit: just a few more niceties and you're *done*.

Negotiating Future Contact

Most guests, as they leave, will suggest that you get together one-on-one in the near future. Unless the guest is a close friend, this almost surely will not happen. You will not see most of these people again for several weeks, or even months. If you live in Los Angeles, make that a year. Longer if you live on opposite sides of the 405 freeway.

Also, at this point in the evening, guests who are not already your friends may suggest you exchange contact information, so you can "hang out again some-time." Use the following scale to gauge the likelihood of this ever occurring.

LIKELY: The guest personally enters your phone number *and* email into their phone, and tells you about a specific event to which they want to invite you within the next month.

SOMEWHAT LIKELY: They assure you they'll friend you on Facebook, and an hour after the party they actually do.

UNLIKELY: They urge *you* to friend *them* on Facebook.

NEVER: They give you what is obviously their work email and tell you to "keep in touch."

Hugging Out

At the beginning of your party, you may have greeted guests with *either* hugs or handshakes. Hugs for old pals and family, handshakes for people you've never met before or don't know well.

But here at the end of the party, there is no such need for equivocation: everyone hugs. Yes, this also applies in the Midwest, where even a hand-

shake feels like a breach of personal space so painfully intimate you might as well be having intercourse. Sorry, get over it. There is too much gray area, too much gnashing of teeth over the hug-versus-handshake question. We're calling it for universal night-ending hugs. Humanity needs hugs.

Exceptions:

1) If a guest is storming out of your party in anger, or you're kicking them out for being a jerkface, a terse handshake or grudging wave goodbye is the *maximum* contact expected.
2) If a guest gives you a romantic vibe, and you want to make it perfectly but politely clear you don't want to sleep with them, a handshake does the trick. Heads up, flirty guest: If the host shakes your hand goodbye, they're not interested.[8]

Cheek Kisses

In parts of Europe, the Middle East, Africa, and Latin America, saying hello *or* goodbye involves a perplexing amount of cheek kissing.

Sometimes planting the lips right on the cheek. Sometimes placing cheek to cheek and kissing air. Sometimes one kiss. Sometimes one kiss for each cheek. Sometimes back and forth between both cheeks, *twice,* for a total of four. We have no doubt that right now, somewhere in Italy, a couple of impeccably dressed dudes, leaning up against their Vespas, between gorgeously cinematic drags off cigarettes which somehow don't give them cancer, are perfecting the twenty-cheek kiss.

But those moves are for professionals. The rest of us are still coming to terms with hugs. So do the kissing thing if a guest starts it, but don't initiate

---

8   *Unless,* flirty guest, you are at the party with your significant other, but you and the host have been flirting all night anyway. In which case the conspicuous goodbye hand-shake is actually an indication that the host *is* hot for you but doesn't want to hug you in front of your dude/lady. Ooh, the sexual tension: isn't it *delicious??*

it, unless you're keen to end the evening by accidentally cracking someone's skull open, or by giving yourself whiplash.

AND FINALLY, A GOODBYE PRIMER

Speaking of Europe, you've likely heard of the French exit, a.k.a. the Irish goodbye, a.k.a. ghosting. It's when a guest sneaks out of the party without telling anyone.

We don't advocate this move, since one of the few tangible rewards a host gets for throwing a dinner party is a "Thank you" for a job well done. On the other hand, it does mean there's one less guest with artichoke dip breath you have to hug goodbye.

In any case, as a host, you should be prepared for this and several other forms of potential guest exits.

The Jewish Goodbye—a.k.a. the Midwestern Goodbye: Wherein everyone at the party hugs each other goodbye, and then they all hang out on your front porch talking for another hour.

The Boston Goodbye: In which your drunk best friend hugs you goodbye, and then you both fall to the ground and start wrestling, and no one knows if you're fighting or what.

The College Goodbye: While everyone's at the front door hugging goodbye, a guest sneaks into the kitchen, steals back the unopened booze they brought to your party, and splits through the back door.

The Jar Jar Binks Goodbye: You hug everyone goodbye. Then you return to the living room to find that the most uninteresting guest at the party is still there, eager to hang out with you some more. No matter how many hints you drop, he fails to realize everything would be better if he were gone.

The British Goodbye: This is when you think a guest pulled an Irish goodbye on you, but it turns out they're just passed out in the backyard.

The New York Goodbye: Five minutes before the party begins, a guest sends you a text saying she can't make it, she knows she's the worst, but let's catch up soon.

The Los Angeles Goodbye: This is when two guests hug you and each other goodbye...and then realize their cars are both parked near each other. So they have to awkwardly walk two blocks together before hugging goodbye again.

Is everyone gone?

Smile.

Clean what you can.

Drink whatever liquid is left in any glass on your path to your bedroom. Sleep.

Wake up. Survey the wreckage. Take yourself to brunch.

Acknowledgments

BRENDAN AND RICO WOULD LIKE TO THANK

The Radio People: American Public Media; our amazing, intrepid, and endlessly calm senior producer, Jackson Musker; DPD staffers James Kim, Khrista Rypl, and Kristina Lopez; our longtime "voice of history," Michelle Philippe; as well as Peter Clowney, Larissa Anderson, Steve Nelson, Eva Fryscak, David Brancaccio, Brittany Martin, Tracey Samuelson, all our interns past and present, Jon Cohn, Kai Ryssdal, Jeff Hnilicka, all the fearless public radio program directors who carry the show, and Deb Clark, Bill Davis, Sarah Lutman, John Rabe, and J.J. Yore—all of whom first had faith.

The Book People: The immensely patient Lindsay Edgecombe and everyone at Levine/Greenberg/Rostan; our talented and well-bearded editor, Michael Szczerban, as well as Nicky Guerreiro, Zea Moscone, Ben Allen, and all at Little, Brown; and Fanny Blanc who made us want to attend the dinner parties in her pictures.

And the People People: Reyhan Harmanci, Danielle Henderson, Richard Lawson, Rebecca Lehrer and Amy S. Choi, Erin McCann, Helen Zaltzman, Christina Rentz, Sadie Stein, Colin Anderson, Michael Del-Grosso, DJ Chad Brown, Paddy Hirsch, Sean Cole, every guest who ever played in our playground, and most of all the fans, especially the ones who made sure to remind us there were actual people listening and appreciating on the other side of our microphones. You're all invited to our party.

RICO WOULD LIKE TO THANK

Corrina Lesser, to whom I owe my sanity and many great things to come. And Colin and Libby Doty, the Gordons, the Mirendas, the Larsons, the Lessers, Ron Strelecki, the Ministry of Unknown Science (Jason Berlin, Cece Pleasants, Montano Sokolow, Eric Trueheart, Tim Walker), Amilea Mea, Joshua and Heather Joy Kamensky, Apryl Lundsten, Linda Williamson and Robert Keil, Morgan Fahey, Rhino Ryland, Sarah Anthony, Andy Hermann and Rebecca Metz, Liz Hamilton and Jon Zerolnick, J. Ryan Stradal and Brooke Delaney, Deborah Dunn, Beth Kracklauer, Kenn Kostyo and Jenn Bushee, Diana Steenbergen, Saadia Bouzelmad, Klazien Schaap, Andres and Joyce de Lange, Rudolfo Perez, Deb Vankin, Amanda Karkoutly, Abram Himmelstein, the cities of Amsterdam and Pittsburgh, and David and Dara Hyde, for the advice. And those I wish could come over right now: David and Eyad.

BRENDAN WOULD LIKE TO THANK

My dream dinner party guest list: Leanne Shapton, whose unerring eye and bottomless tin of peanuts made this book better. Lauren, Nate, Anna, and Owen Crum; Ryan Alcorn; Marinko, Carlo, and Danielle Stokic; Vladimir and Barbara Salamun; Ezra, Jessie, and Rafa Feinberg; Jessica Chiu; Paul Rodriguez; Clay Weiner; Aya Kanai; Manu Kingston; Lindsey Hamilton; Andrew Weiner; Patrick Hoffman; Chad, Annie, and Dion Brown; Jess Hundley; Manu Kingston; Lyndsey Hamilton; Kristiania Clark; my South 2nd dinner party companions: Robin, Bernadette, Jodie, Dave, Emma, and Ava; my cooking sensei and friend Jolynn Deloach; Erica Levin; Ethan Kramer; Brad Neely; Andrew Haeg; Aja Pecknold; Jynne Martin; and Laris Kreslins, who in the summer of 2005 told me I should start a podcast. And most importantly my *baka*, Greta Salamun, whose love of food, entertaining, and Scotch in her coffee awed and inspired me, and my *dida*, Anthony Salamun, who is my lodestar, and not just because he drank string bean juice straight from the serving bowl, but that was pretty cool, too!

About Us

Brendan and Rico are cocreators, cohosts, and coproducers of *The Dinner Party Download*, a national public radio show and podcast about culture and food produced by American Public Media. It has been downloaded over 26 million times, was awarded an NEA grant, and was named "Best Food Podcast" by the Academy of Podcasters in 2016.

Brendan and Rico were named two of *Food & Wine*'s "Forty Big Food Thinkers Forty and Under" and appeared as judges on *Top Chef Masters*. In addition to producing *The Dinner Party Download*, they each write food, design, and travel articles for various national print outlets.

Brendan, based in Brooklyn, holds a JD and loves exploring his mother's native Croatia. Rico, based in Los Angeles, is a native Pittsburgher with an MA in screenwriting from the American Film Institute who has a dangerous love of Amsterdam and vinyl records. They both like gin martinis, but Brendan's is better.

Are we still on this? Mine is better. — RG

Yeah, but mine. — BFN

We agreed to do a joint bio page to avoid fights like this. Also, the better one is mine. — RG

I mean, yes, excluding mine. — BFN

Guys. — Editor

@ricogagliano @bfnewnam